ECOLOGY
&
LIBERATION

ECOLOGY AND JUSTICE SERIES

LEONARDO BOFF

ECOLOGY
&
LIBERATION

A New Paradigm

Translated from the Italian by John Cumming

ORBIS BOOKS

Maryknoll, New York 10545

The Catholic Foreign Mission Society of America (Maryknoll) recruits and trains people for overseas missionary service. Through Orbis Books, Maryknoll aims to foster the international dialogue that is essential to mission. The books published, however, reflect the opinions of their authors and are not meant to represent the official position of the society.

Originally published in Portuguese with the title *Ecologia, Mundialização, Espiritualidade*, copyright © 1993 by Editora Ática, São Paulo, Brazil. The present translation is based on the Italian edition, *Ecologia, Mondialità, Mistica*, copyright © 1993 by Cittadella Editrice, Assisi, Italy.

Library of Congress Cataloguing in Publication Data

Boff, Leonardo.
    [Ecologia, mundialização, espiritualidade. English]
    Ecology and liberation : a new paradigm / Leonardo Boff ; translated from the Italian by John Cumming.
        p.   cm. — (Ecology and justice series)
    Includes index.
    ISBN 0-88344-978-1
    1. Human ecology—Religious aspects—Christianity.   2. Liberation theology. I. Title. II. Series: Ecology and justice.
    BT695.5.B6413   1995
    261.8'362—dc20

                           94-34199
                              CIP

For Pedro and Betto
Marcia and Clotilde
who were true brothers
and sisters to me
when I needed them

Contents

PART 2
FROM ECOLOGY TO GLOBAL CONSCIOUSNESS

PREFACE

Creative Crisis

We live in critical and therefore creative times. The political and ideological map of the world has changed in the last five years. Structures have collapsed and with them many ways of looking at things. But dreams remain. They are an essential part of being human and will always persist. They even allow new visions and furnish the enthusiasm needed for thought and creativity.

But dreams always bring much pain with them. Many people have lost their guiding principle. Others are inwardly shattered and cannot come to terms with the fading of so many ample prospects. They live only because they are not yet dead. But the springs of hope within them are almost entirely dry. Suffering, strange to say, sets the mind to work.

The pieces collected in this volume were composed in the last two years, under the influence of precipitate and momentous political upheavals that have affected the author's life too. But he has only taken a different route. He has not changed direction. He has jumped into another trench, but he has not left the frontline. The struggle continues.

These reflections are the fruit of crisis, which always has a purifying effect. Like a crucible, it frees gold from mineral impurities. The good part of the trunk is laid bare and can now be used to build with.

These pieces, then, are testimonies charged with hope. The knapsack still contains some provisions for the way before us.

There is still enough water in the flask for a good stretch of the road. We can move ahead. The fire is still burning and enables us to see the right direction to take. Not a word need be uttered, and we know how to sing without speaking. This is the mystical way.

Rio de Janeiro, Vale Encantado
October 12, 1992—the day of the resistance
and of the liberation of AfroIndioLatin America

A Sermon from the Mount of Corcovado

In those days the Christ of Corcovado, in the city of St. Sebastian de Janeiro, shuddered and came to life again. The former cement and stone now turned to flesh and blood. With outspread arms, as if to embrace the city and the world, he opened his mouth and said:*

"I feel compassion for you, millions and millions of little sisters and brothers, exiled from the land, alone, scattered in the forest, pushed to the periphery, fallen by the wayside on so many streets without any Samaritan to help you.

"You are all blessed, all you who are poor, hungry, sick and without hope. You are oppressed and victims of a corrupt society, so how can I expect you to live a life of perfect virtue or upbraid you for all your imperfections?

"My Father who is the lord and giver of life treasures you all in his very heart. You will form the basis of his kingdom of life, justice, love, and freedom. For me, your oaths and blasphemies are neither of these things, but cries for help that pierce and rend the heart. For me, your individualism is not egotism

---

*The Christ of Corcovado is the famous statue of the Savior dominating Guanabara Bay in Rio de Janeiro.

but an unyielding desire to survive. Your terrible pain and suffering have lasted longer than my own. You realize and perpetuate throughout the centuries my own saving passion.

"Heaven help you, masters of power, who have sucked the workers' blood for five hundred years. You have reduced them to the level of cheap fuel so that the machines you own can bring you the profits of injustice.

"You have used my holy name to legitimize your order, which can scarcely be said to help the people to progress.

"O perverse generation, when will you cease trying the patience of my suffering servants? The exterminating angel of God's own justice, who has already descended throughout history, hovers above your enterprise.

"Neither I nor my Father will try your case but the victims of your actions.

"Look into their eyes and study their faces! I shall be there in your judges.

"There is only one way for you to save yourselves, and that is to join the struggle of the oppressed for bread, freedom, tenderness, and beauty, which are not only for them but for you and for everyone!

"Blessed and vast lands of Latin America! It is my great desire that amid all the nations, among all these nations of God, you will express my hospitality and geniality, my love of life, my openness and lack of calculation, and my humanitarian grace and that of your heavenly Father.

"Watch over the forests and mountains, the great Cordigliera and the banks of the Amazon, the rivers flowing with water and the deep valleys, the wild animals and the many varieties of birds. They are all your brothers and sisters.

"Curb your greed. Care for them as my Father cares for them. They will inherit the kingdom. They will be transfigured and will live for ever together with you, with me, and with the Spirit of life in the Father's kingdom.

"You are blessed, Native American Indians, my first witnesses in that rich land of Abya Yala. Your city, your pyramids, your long streets, your rites, the sun and the moon that you honor, are signs of the true God, the God who is far and near, of the God through whom all have life. You will not lack his forgiveness for the wars which you made to ensure the human (but inhuman) sacrifices you offered.

"Woe to those who subjugated you, who destroyed your culture, who consumed your flowers, who tried to castrate the sun, who threw down your altars, who imposed their own teachings on you, day and night, with the violence of the cross and the sword.

"Blessed are those among you who believe in the hidden strength of the seed. You have the power to raise up the people and to give back life to their culture, bringing joy to the aged and praising my holy name: God, Virachocha, and Quetzalcoátl.

"Blessed and even more blessed are you, my black brothers and sisters, always subject to the injustice of slavery. The historical humiliation that you have suffered has made you especially dear to the heart of your heavenly Father. You are the suffering servant present in history, who liberates through suffering, redeems with blood, and saves with the cross. You yourselves are unaware of the immense benefits you have brought to all humankind through the wickedness you have suffered and resisted without losing your faith, singing, dancing and dreaming of the Promised Land. You are entitled, right up to the last day, to lay claim to your rights, and to obtain recognition, freedom, and a full life.

"Accursed the slave huts where you were held. Accursed the pillories and platforms where you were displayed. Accursed a thousand times the whip with which you were beaten. Accursed for all time the chains you bore.

"Blessed the hiding place of runaway slaves, the cap of liberty, the advent of a world of brothers and sisters, the sign of the kingdom of heaven.

"Blessed those who fight for the earth in the country, so that they can work to turn the land into the banquet table where the world's hunger can be satisfied. Blessed those who fight for the earth in the city, so that they can live with the dignity of sons and daughters of God.

"Accursed the thief who steals the land that the Father has destined for all human beings and kills the peasants, my brothers and sisters. Truly I tell you, you will be stripped of everything. If you do not heed my warning, all you will have in the end is the soil weighing on your body in the graveyard. Blessed are you, women of the people who refuse ever to surrender and who fight for a new society in which men and women together, individually and in solidarity, will inaugurate a fraternal and sisterly alliance.

"Blessed are you, millions of needy and deserted children, the children of the streets, victims of an atrocious society that shuts you out and which the Father loathes. He will wipe away all your tears. He will embrace you and play with you forever, for once upon a time his son Jesus was a child too, and they said they would kill Jesus, so he had to take refuge in Egypt.

"Blessed are the ministers, bishops, priests, religious, and community workers who humbly serve the people, among the people, and with the people.

"Woe betide those who turn their backs on the people and pretend to speak on their behalf, who use their staffs to beat their little sheep but not to drive away the wolves who seek to devour them. I shall not recognize them and speak for them when they appear before my Father.

"Blessed are the base communities, whether they serve the life and faith of the poor, or celebrate his name, establish good will, and offer new hope of a purpose in living and dying.

"Blessed the movements that seek the liberation of all people, above all the oppressed and marginalized. Theirs is the same cause for which I lived, suffered, was crucified, and rose again, in order to bring about a new world in which light conquers darkness and life is worth more than material things. No one who was a member of my party and spoke on my behalf will suffer abuse. You are my disciples and you are close to me.

"Blessed are those who seek new ways to survive, new forms of production, of communitarian distribution, of consumption by sharing. I assure you that I travel with you and that you will always find new forms of living together.

"Blessed are those who in the midst of suffering look forward to the great dawn of liberation and to the fruits of divine grace and human effort, for their eyes shall see the sun of justice shine forth. Blessed are those who will not allow good will to fade away, who keep their inward fire going and still believe in the dream of a new world.

"Blessed are those who do everything possible and furthermore dare to try to bring about some small part of the impossible. You will experience the realization of the hope which is indispensable in life. Truly, truly I say unto you: you will be truly happy because in this way you will bring happiness to my sons and daughters, and you will already be travelling along the road to the kingdom you are helping to build. Only thus will it be yours and mine forever."

PART 1

ECOLOGY:
A NEW PARADIGM

Ecology has to do with the relations, interaction, and dialogue of all living creatures (whether alive or not) among themselves and with all that exists. This includes not only nature (natural ecology) but culture and society (human ecology, social ecology, and so on). From an ecological viewpoint everything that exists, co-exists. Everything that co-exists, pre-exists. And everything that co-exists and pre-exists subsists by means of an infinite web of all-inclusive relations. Nothing exists outside relationships. Ecology reaffirms the interdependence of beings, interprets all hierarchies as a matter of function, and repudiates the so-called right of the strongest. All creatures manifest and possess their own relative autonomy; nothing is superfluous or marginal. All being constitutes a link in the vast cosmic chain. As Christians, we may say that it comes from God and returns to God.

Ecology is not an expensive whim of the rich, something trendy restricted to ecological groups, or to the Greens and their respective political parties. The ecological question has to do with reaching a new level of globalization, of world awareness and conscience, where there is a universal under-standing of the importance of the earth as a whole, the welfare of nature and of humankind, the interdependence of all, and of the apocalyptic catastrophe menacing all creation.

CHAPTER 1

Ecology

Politics, Theology, and Mysticism

The term *ecology* was coined in 1866 by the German biologist Ernst Haeckel (1834-1919). It derives from two Greek words, *oikos*, which means "house" or "home," and *logos*, meaning "reflection" or "study." Therefore *ecology* means the study of the conditions and relations that make up the habitat (the house) of each and every person and, indeed, organism in nature. According to Haeckel's definition, "Ecology is the study of the interdependence and interaction of living organisms (animals and plants) and their environment (inanimate matter)."

Ecology: The Science and Art of Interaction

Nowadays the term's reference has been extended to cover all living things. Ecology stands for the relations, interaction, and dialogue of all existing creatures (whether alive or not) among themselves and with all that exists. Nature (all living things as a whole), from elementary particles and primordial energy all the way to more complex forms of life, is dynamic; it comprises an intricate network of connections on all sides.

Ecology encompasses not only nature (natural ecology) but culture and society (human ecology, social ecology, and so on).

Thus we have subsidiary fields of ecology such as urban ecology, health ecology, mental ecology, and so forth. It is important, therefore, to understand that ecology tries to point out the bonds uniting all natural and cultural organisms; it stresses the interdependence of the various elements in the network of phenomena that constitutes the ecological totality. The latter does not, of course, imply an unchangeable standardization and homogenization, or the sum of many parts and details, but may be said to form an infinitely rich and diverse dynamic unity.

Consequently, the basic concept of nature seen from an ecological standpoint is that everything is related to everything else in all respects. A slug on the roadway is related to the most distant galaxy. A flower is related to the great explosion fifteen billion years ago. The carbon monoxide in the exhaust gases from a bus is related to our Milky Way. My own consciousness is related to elementary subatomic particles.

At the human level, ecology is an attempt to relate everything that occurs laterally and horizontally, and to overcome the situation of, as it were, blinkered scholars and scientists who are aware only of the knowledge in their own specific field (the doctor who knows nothing but medicine; the economist who knows only economics; and the priest who knows nothing but religion). We have to develop an interdisciplinary understanding of things. Ecology also tries to put everything into relation with the past, to see things in the context of their genealogy, for they have had a long history of billions of years before reaching their present form. In this way ecology tries to avoid a simplistic, fixed, and fundamentalist view of things. It also tries to look ahead. Just as they have a past, so all things have a future and are oriented to that future. It is important to avoid focusing exclusively on the immediate present and on our own generation. We must develop a form of solidarity with the generations that are as yet unborn (generational solidarity), ensuring the common inheritance of a healthy natural world. Finally, ecology seeks a vision of the whole which does not derive from the sum of the parts but from the organic interdependence of everything with everything else. It thus seeks to overcome the dominant way of thinking, which is too analytical and not synthetic enough, because it is insufficiently in touch with other forms of experience and ways of looking at reality.

This basic ecological approach is known as "holism" or the "holistic approach." *Holism* comes from the Greek *holos*, which means "totality" (and is a term that was more widely diffused from 1926 onward after its use by South African philosopher Jan Smuts). It means the tendency in nature to form wholes that are more than the sum of the parts. Here we have a synthesis that orders, organizes, regulates, and completes the parts in a whole, and relates each whole to another, even greater whole. Holistic ecology as a practice and theory comprises and relates all existents one to another and with the environment in the perspective of the infinitely small elementary particles (quarks), of the infinitely large instances of the realms of cosmic space, of the infinitely complex systems of life, of the infinite profundity of the human heart, and of the infinite mystery of the boundless oceans of primordial energy from which everything emanates (the infinite void that is also the image of God).

Thus we may define ecology as the science and art of relations and of related beings. The home/habitat/*oikos*, in fact, is made up of living beings, matter, energy, bodies, and forces in permanent relation to one another. In this perspective we may say that ecology is eminently theological by nature. As Christians, we say that God is a Trinity, the eternal relationship of the three divine Persons, the infinite communion of Father, Son, and Holy Spirit (*perichoresis*). The entire universe emanates from this divine relational interplay and is made in the image and likeness of the Trinity.

For Haeckel, a hundred years ago, ecology was a branch of biology. It was a subsection of a natural science. Today, for us, it represents a global interest, a question of life and death of humankind and of the whole planetary system. It is the problem of problems, and indeed the question that makes relative all other questions and constitutes the new radicality as well as the actual core of human preoccupations.

All earthly creatures are threatened, beginning with the poor and the marginalized. This time it will not be a Noah's ark that will save the fortunate few, leaving all others to perish. Because of its cardinal importance, all human activity and all science should focus on ecology and make their specific contributions to the preservation of the creation. To answer ecological conundrums it is not enough just to stick the particle "eco" in front of just any science, as in eco-economics, eco-sociology, eco-politics, eco-psychology, eco-theology, and so forth, and then to carry on exactly as before. We need a strict form of self-criticism. We have to decide to what extent this or that science is a factor of ecological imbalance, this or that policy leads to the degradation of the environment, and this or that model of development is an instrument by which nature is plundered. We have to delve deeper and discover to what extent this or that science has to be developed within an ecological perspective if it is to become a major factor in the protection, respect, and promotion of nature. Today, this process of reconversion is incumbent on everyone.

A Necessary Answer to Common Objections

On the basis of these initial considerations, it is not difficult to answer the objections commonly raised against ecological interests.

"Ecology is a luxury of the rich. It is a product of the northern hemisphere. These people have despoiled nature in their own countries and have robbed the colonized peoples of the entire world, and after all that are now claiming a safe ambience and ecological reserve for the preservation of a species in the process of decline." This is true. The industrialized nations, almost all located in the northern hemisphere, are responsible for 80 percent of the pollution of the earth (the United States alone for 23 percent). But today the problem is global and no longer regional. In a sense, ecological awareness is a luxury of the rich, for they have managed to avoid the injurious effects of their kind of society and of the developments that it has given rise to. But that does not mean that the problem does not exist. The solutions suggested in such societies are indeed short-sighted (conservationism, environmentalism), and they do not critically scrutinize the actual model of society and the paradigms of development and consumption (social ecology, deep ecology, holistic ecology) that are the main causes of the worldwide ecological crisis, especially the bad health and premature death of the poor.

Josué de Castro rightly says: "Poverty is our main environmental problem." We have to face up to the problem that has begun to stir the conscience of the rich, but to conceive it appropriately and to proffer a different solution that respects the interests of all human beings and of nature, starting from the fate of the most threatened persons and creatures. The mistake of the rich is traditional; it consists in thinking only of themselves and in lacking a holistic perspective that embraces everything and everyone. They are environmentalists who want fewer human beings in the environment, claiming that that will make things better, for humans pollute and destroy it. Or they are conservationists who wish to conserve threatened vegetable and animal species in a special reserve. Ecological behavior and attitudes are to prevail in this area, whereas outside it modern human beings will continue to behave selfishly and carry on their plunder. What we have here is a collectively egotistical and self-interested vision that does not deserve to be called ecological, above all because it does not include the most complex and also most responsible of created beings, the human being.

"Ecology is a product and interest of ecological groups, a form of discourse practiced by experts specializing in botany, tropical forests, oceanography, biology, genetics, and so on—people who

do not concern themselves with social problems." In fact, the ecological question is too universal to be relegated to specialized
groups. Such groups certainly have undeniable merits. Nevertheless, it is impossible to develop an adequate respect for nature
without taking into account the way in which nature adversely
affects important creatures, such as marginalized and impoverished human beings. This situation of social injustice includes an
element of ecological injustice, and vice versa. In this case, too,
the original understanding of ecology is maintained: that which
is concerned not only with animals, plants, and the purity of the
atmosphere, but with the joint and global relations of human beings and nature. The authentic notion of ecology is always holistic and maintains an alliance of solidarity with nature.

"Ecology is a special concern of Greens and their respective political parties, who are often romantic and stand apart
from the class struggle and the revolutionary project of the
oppressed." The Greens deserve praise for their action in taking into the political field the questions of environmental pollution, and the wretched quality of life in the industrial and
urban world. They are organized in the form of political parties in order to give their concern an effective voice when confronted with the indifference of the other parties, even though
their cause is of general interest. The Greens are also interested in sustaining an ecological critique of the economy, and
of the politics and of the type of society based on the indis-
criminate exploitation of natural resources. With the growth
of ecological awareness there will no longer be any need for
Green parties. Nevertheless, it would be foolish to imagine
that ecology makes other forms of social antagonism obsolete.
It would be disastrous, in the name of ecology, to forget the
workers' struggle and the validity of strikes. Ecological concern insists that the struggle of the working class is not a matter only of a better wage (corporative interests) but of a better
quality of life and labor, of a different type of society and a
new model of development that includes social welfare and
the welfare of nature (collective well-being).

The ecological question leads to a new level of global aware-ness: the importance of the earth as a whole, the common good of nature and of humankind, the interdependence of all, and the apocalyptic dangers that threaten the creation. Human be-ings include homicidal and genocidal individuals, as history has shown, and also biocidal, ecocidal, and geocidal persons.

Our common home is deeply cleft from top to bottom. It could collapse. How are we to repair it? Are we merely to fill the cracks with mortar and cover up with a spot of whitewash? What if the real reason for the decay eats away at the very foundations of the subsiding house? Surely we should get to the bottom of things and try to save the entire house, together with all those who live in it? Our examination of the problem should proceed along these lines.

Human Beings: Guardian Angels or Demons of the Earth?

The report of the U.S. Worldwatch Institute is especially prominent among the various surveys of the environmental crisis. From 1984 it has published a detailed annual account of the world situation with special reference to progress toward a sustainable society.

The predictions are alarming. Between 1500 and 1850 one species was eliminated every ten years. Between 1850 and 1950 the rate was one a year. In 1990 ten species a day were disap-pearing. By the year 2000 one species will be vanishing every hour. The species mortality rate is speeding up constantly. Be-tween 1975 and 2000 20 percent of all living species will have disappeared.

Since 1950 we have lost a fifth of the cultivatable surface and of the tropical rain forests. Every year we lose twenty-five million tons of humus through erosion, salination, and deserti-fication. This corresponds to an area as big as the Caribbean region, excluding Cuba. The forests of the world are vanishing at a rate of twenty million hectares a year. According to the calculation of the IBGE (1988) 5 percent of the Amazonian forests have already been destroyed. Other estimates make it 12 percent. But percentages can be deceptive. One percent of the Amazon corresponds to forty thousand square kilometers, or rather four million hectares. Up to 1970 five million hectares were deforested. From 1970 to 1988, in a period of eighteen years, twenty million hectares were deforested. The denuded area is equal to the entire area of Brazil sown with soya, millet, and wheat.

Latin America accounts for 12 percent of the earth's surface and alone possesses two-thirds of all the world's plant species. There are some thirty to fifty million species of insects. Deforestation will have removed thirty to fifty thousand species by the year 2000. Most Brazilians today live in conditions far worse than when deforestation began; no advantage has been gained from laying waste the forests.

The main global problems associated with the environment are acid rain, atmospheric pollution, the destruction of the ozone layer, deforestation/desertification, and overpopulation.

Acid rain derives from uncontrolled industrialization. Sulphur dioxide and nitrogen oxide in the atmosphere are transformed into acidic particles deposited on vegetation, in rivers and lakes, causing contamination of foodstuffs and respiratory diseases in living beings. Every day about 650 million people are exposed to harmful amounts of sulphur dioxide. The fish have disappeared from thirteen thousand square kilometers of Norwegian waters. Aquatic life has vanished from fourteen thousand Swedish lakes. Thirty-five percent of European forests are seriously affected by acid rain.

The greenhouse effect and atmospheric pollution result from the consumption of fossil fuels (oil and coal), which give off carbon dioxide and other gases. This fact, together with the ongoing deforestation (with chlorophyll photosynthesis from vegetation absorbing carbon dioxide), produces a greenhouse effect leading to atmospheric pollution. Last century the temperature increased by 0.6 degrees Centigrade. In the next hundred years we may expect an increase of 1.5 to 5.5 degrees Centigrade. This could provoke incalculable disasters linked to drought and to the melting of the polar icecaps. If the ocean rises by a single meter, 10 percent of Bangladesh will be flooded, leading to the flight of eight million inhabitants. Many animals and plants are unable to adapt and will disappear.

The ozone layer is a stratum of the atmosphere thirty to fifty kilometers above the earth's surface; it protects life from the ultraviolet radiation responsible for skin cancer and the collapse of the immune system. The emission into the atmosphere of industrial chemicals (CFCs), found in dry-cleaning solvents, sprays, and various insecticides, leads to the destruction of the ozone layer. It is estimated that for each percentage point of reduction in the ozone layer, in the United States alone there are ten thousand new cases of skin cancer.

The main contaminators of the planet are the rich and industrialized countries. In 1985 the United States released into the atmosphere over one billion tons of carbon dioxide. The former Soviet Union emitted 985 million tons. The result is paradoxical and hypocritical: While the countries of the northern hemisphere are the main nations responsible for the global ecological crisis, they are also the countries that are unwilling to take on the main responsibility for correcting the destructive processes. Instead, they seek to impose the burden of helping nature to recover on countries in the southern hemisphere. This was made clear at the Second International Conference on Ecology and Development, held under the aegis of the United Nations, in Rio de Janeiro in June 1992. Surely those who have most harmed the earth should contribute most to its repair?

The population of the world is growing at an alarming rate. In 1950 there were two and a half billion people in the world. In 1975 there were almost four billion. In 1990 there were 5.2 billion. In 2000 there will be 6.1 billion. It took humankind ten thousand generations to get to two billion inhabitants. Now only one generation is needed to move from two to five billion. Will the earth's ecosystem be able to sustain so many people? The growth rate in the Third World is about 3 to 4 percent a year and can feed about 1.3 percent. Two-thirds of the world's population are poor. Sixty million die from hunger and sickness associated with poverty; twenty million of them are children.

These data give some idea of the size of the global crisis of our planetary system. Gaia (a Greek term for the earth conceived as an immense living being) is sick and wounded. Human beings, especially with the advent of the industrial revolution, have proved that they are exterminating angels, veritable demons of the earth. But human beings could also become guardian angels, intent upon saving the earth, which is their fatherland and motherland.

Astronauts who travelled into space and recorded their impressions of the earth described it as a ship on a voyage. In fact, in this ship which is the earth a fifth of the population are travelling in first class and in luxury class; they enjoy all the benefits. They consume 80 percent of the resources available for the voyage. The remaining 80 percent of the passengers are travelling steerage. They suffer cold, hunger, and all kinds of privations. Many ask why they are travelling steerage. Need forces others to rebel. It is not difficult to see what is at stake. Either everyone can be saved in a system of communal solidarity and participation on the ship—and in that case fundamental changes are necessary—or, as a result of outrage and revolt, the ship will explode and throw everyone into the sea. This awareness is growing throughout the world.

There is a global danger. We need a global solution and salvation. For that to happen we need a global revolution and an integral liberation. Ecology is the attempted answer to this global life-and-death problem. How are we to put into practice a kind of ecology that will safeguard the natural and cultural creation in justice, solidarity, and peace?

Ecology, Its Projects and Practice

Worldwide society is becoming more conscious of the implications of ecological disaster on a planetary level. An ecological culture is slowly growing with forms of behavior and practices that embody a vision of the world as a whole and thus lead to greater concentration and concern in our confrontations with nature. The notion is growing that any attack on the earth is aggression against the sons and daughters of the earth. Mother Earth, the great and generous Pachamama of Andean culture, suffers in her sons and daughters. She is revived by the revolution of feeling and concern. I shall now examine various aspects of this ecological concern.

The Technological Project: Ecotechnology

Ecotechnology starts from the present model of society and the predominant type of development. All modern societies across the world are structured on the axis of economy. But economy in its modern sense has lost its original significance: the administration of the fair and modest means necessary for life and well-being. Rational application of scant income is the central activity of most households in the Third World. That is economy in the true sense of the term. But that is not the kind of economics practiced by the institutional economists, who serve a very different conception.

For modern society, whether socialist or liberal bourgeois, economics is the science of limitless growth or, in more technical terms, of the unlimited expansion of productive forces. At the end of each year the country has to show that there has been growth over the previous year. This imperative has given rise to the notion of unlimited growth that, like some incubus, has come to dominate society as a whole for some five hundred years.

The greater the development the less the investments and the greater the profits. The common preconception is that we move within the ambit of two indeterminate quantities: natural resources and progress toward the future. But the harsh fact confirmed in the report of the Club of Rome (1972) on the limits of growth and in all successive documents (especially the annual reports on the state of the earth) is this: the two quantities are illusory. The natural resources are limited and nonrenewable, and the present model of progress is not applicable on a universal level. If China thought of giving Chinese families the automobiles owned by North American families (about two to a family), the country would be paralyzed immediately, if only because of the excess vehicles on the streets and the lack of fuel.

The model of unlimited growth is possessed by a demon: it is constructed only on the basis of the exploitation of the working classes, on the underdevelopment of dependent nations, and on the rape of nature. The result is that economic development does not give rise to simultaneous social development. The benefits are available only to a restricted group of nations or to the upper classes of a nation, and they do not include the well-being of nature.

What is the point of the technological project? It maintains intact the model of society and the corresponding paradigm of development, but it proposes techniques and procedures that favor the conservation of the environment and the reduction of any undesirable effects of the models in question.

There are such appropriate technological devices as filtration of noxious gases, noise reduction, and the decontamination of rivers and lakes. Such projects have to be studied and advanced, so that the technology that has devastated nature can also contribute to its cure. But it is not enough to attack the consequences and to ignore the causes. That is tantamount to grinding down the wolf's teeth without changing his wolfish nature. In other words, it is hardly efficacious to work out remedies and to leave the cause of the illness untreated. We lack a fundamental critique of a model of society that would promote a sustainable kind of ecological development.

The Political Project: Ecopolitics

Politics has to do with power and the control of the common good. Human beings have needs, interests, and desires. Power decides access to necessities, the satisfaction of class interests and of desires. Want is structurally infinite. It discovers a limit in solidarity, which persuades it to renounce things for the sake of others' right to live and enjoy nature. We live and suffer within the framework of a society divided into classes that produce the means of power and life unequally and distribute them asymmetrically.

The dominant class does not set limits to its own desires, but demands that others should satisfy their wants from their own resources, even when such needs are only the requirements of necessity. Poverty, like riches, produces ecological imbalances. When constrained by need, the poor exhaust for the sake of short-term satisfaction what might be their long-term support (deforestation, throwing garbage into valleys, hunting and fishing without any thought of compensating resources, and so forth). The rich waste resources that the poor are without today and that generations of humans will be without tomorrow. Mahatma Gandhi rightly said: "The earth satisfies the needs of all, but not the greed of those bent on insane consumption."

In the present situation, those who hold power control politics in order to guarantee their own interests and to satisfy their own desires. Entrepreneurial groups and blocs work out their development plans according to an ideology governed by their own advantage and the profit motive. They have to follow the logic of their system or give way to the forceful strategies of their competitors. The state, in turn, pursues its own policy of industrial, energy, agricultural, road, urban, and other forms of development, applying the same criteria in an overall system. The price paid for all these endeavors is the aggressive use of the ecosystem (atmospheric pollution, destruction of the countryside, and so forth).

Under the pressure of the new awareness, however, development policy can be affected by attempts to establish some kind of equilibrium between the demands of progress and ecological damage. Even if there is no clear renunciation of the modern paradigm of unlimited development, and the internal contradictions, asymmetry, and oppositions, divisions and antagonisms continue unabated, people are aware of the ecological question, which is now so plain to see that lip service at least must be paid to it.

Clearly, however, there is no real attempt in present-day ecopolitics to redefine development from the very basis up, as ecological awareness really demands. Moreover, it is also necessary to plan and introduce an ecologically sustainable form of development adapted to regional ecosystems (for example, the natural resource policy of Chico Mendes, which was appropriate to the Amazonian ecosystem). We do indeed find the ruling metaphor of "sustainable development" in official documents. (*Sustainable development* was defined by the UN Brundtland Commission in 1987 as "that development which takes into account present needs without compromising the possibility of future generations satisfying their own needs.") In the last analysis, however, it is always development itself that counts, even at the cost of ecological disorder. When a conflict arises between development and ecology, the decision is usually taken in favor of development at the cost of ecology. It would seem that capitalist greed is incompatible with the conservation of nature.

It is important to emphasize the progress of ecopolitics in respect to establishing simple forms of ecotechnology. Consideration of ecological factors has contributed to the improvement of the quality of life in transport, nutrition, dwelling places, and so forth. The term *ecodevelopment* has been coined in this regard. It refers to a form of development that always takes the ecological factor into account. A policy of this kind affirms that nature too comprises a form of capital along with the means of production and labor. It is as important to contribute to the reproduction of nature as to ensure that the interests of the work force are safeguarded.

But we are still faced with the basic question of the social order. What kind of society do we want? Surely we want it to be more participatory, egalitarian, aiming at solidarity, and capable of uniting imagination and analytical reason, fantasy and logic, technology and utopia. But do we want a society that is more integrated in and with nature? For the marginalized sector of the population (in the peripheral countries the majority), what does it mean to say that foodstuffs should be organic and additive-free when they haven't enough to eat anyway? What meaning is there in a policy of devoting public means to natural gas when there are no public funds anyway? Is it sufficient to offer the children in the *favelas* enriched milk when they lack any form of basic health care? We are without a global policy regarding an ecological framework capable of safeguarding all appropriate aspects of social ecology; that is what is really needed, rather than mere sporadic interventions which essentially benefit only elite groups and no others.

As I have already insisted, development policy should be appropriate to the regional ecosystem. The pharaonic projects of Henry Ford for rubber exploitation in Amazonia in 1927, and, fifty years later, those of Daniel Ludwig for cellulose and timber in Jari, and, finally, the Volkswagen projects of the 1970s, resulted in vast failures, because they did not take any account whatsoever of the ecological question. All this has been at the expense of two million hectares of forest, in the case of the Jari project; and 144,000 hectares destroyed in the case of Volkswagen in order to feed forty-six thousand head of cattle (an incredible thirty thousand square meters devoted to each head). The gigantic nature of such projects reveals the irrationality of the development model being followed and the need to replace it with a more holistic vision that also takes the ecological aspect into account.

The Social Project: Social Ecology

Today, in reality, it is not so much the development model that is in a state of crisis as the dominant type of society in the world. After all, the development model is worked out within this particular form of society. The particular society decides on its own type of development. But that is not the whole story.

All earthly societies—even though there are some that enjoy a more caring relationship with nature and therefore deserve to be valued more highly—consume energy. The problem is no new one but is thousands of years old. Both the external world and the mental structure of every human being are marked by it. Even as far back as the neolithic period (8-10 million years B.C.E.), with the rise of agriculture and the origins of the city, we find the first traces of the abuse of nature. But from the sixteenth century, with the advent of mercantile and then industrial society, the project of systematic exploitation of nature based on positions of power really took hold. With the growth of domination through the application of science and technology, the destruction of the environment began to take place on a massive scale.

Today the ravages are on a planetary scale, affecting adversely soil, air, water, climate, flora, fauna, and the global quality of human life. The 21,500 cities with some eight to twelve million inhabitants, are veritable purgatories, when they are not ecological hells.

As I have already remarked, the axis on which a modern society turns is its economy, seen as the whole set of powers and tools for creating wealth; this means nature and other human beings are exploited. Through the economics of growth, nature is degraded to the level of mere "natural resources," or "raw materials," at the disposal of humankind. Workers are seen as "human resources" and as a mere function of production. Everything is governed by an instrumental and mechanistic vision: persons, animals, plants, minerals. All creatures, in short, lose their relative autonomy and their intrinsic value.

They are reduced to the level of mere means to an end, which human beings, seen as the rulers of the universe and the center of all interests, are free to decide.

In this paradigm, the relation between humanity and nature is one of continuous warfare. The equilibrium between development and ecology is, in reality, no more than a truce. The destructive logic inherent in the process of quantitative development is not cancelled but merely redefined. A truce is established in order to allow nature to recover (natural time is much slower than the quick, all too quick, time of technology), and accordingly nature once again falls victim to the greed of developmental logic.

We also have to understand the perverse logic that justifies the precise degree and type of social order needed to guarantee the production of goods and privileges for only a section of society. Others benefit from these things only in a subordinate form, without having a voice in defining the meaning and direction of social life. The same power is used to direct and mold nature so that it yields up its goods for unequal distribution. The same logic of domination is used for people and for nature. C. S. Lewis rightly said that what we call human power over nature has actually become the power exercised by some people over others, using nature as a tool. Social injustice leads to ecological injustice, and vice versa.

This social model is heavily dualistic. It makes distinctions between persons and nature, man and woman, masculine and feminine, God and world, body and spirit, sex and tenderness. This vision always benefits one of the poles, giving rise to hierarchy and subordinating one of the two terms involved. In our case we have a society with a patriarchal structure. This is a form of monotheism (just one God), which makes its appearance in monarchical and non-trinitarian terms opposed to the idea of communion.

This is a fragmentary, myopic, and erroneous vision. It does not acknowledge the differences to be found within a vast overall unity and the interdependence between society and environment. The human being is the result of a long cosmic and biological process; without elements of nature such as bacteria, viruses, micro-organisms, the genetic code, and the primordial chemical elements, human beings would not exist. They are in a state of continual dialogue with their environment.

An ecological lens enables us to see and describe humankind, men and women, appropriately. The human being is an animal of the mammal class, the order of primates, the family of hominids, the human genus, the species sapiens, with a body of thirty million cells, procreated and controlled by a genetic system produced in the course of a natural evolutionary process of four to five billion years, with a mind capable of forming global visions and constructing an indivisible unity, on the basis of some ten million of his or her ten billion neurones vibrating in unison, in order symbolically to create and recreate the universe and proffer an ultimate and all-inclusive meaning. The movement of the human race has been from the natural world to the personal world, and from the personal to the social and cultural world. In all these phases humankind has always existed in interaction with nature, so that social ecology always has to be appropriately articulated with natural ecology.

Consequently, the individual and social human being is part of nature. The human being belongs to nature just as nature belongs to humankind and depends on human care and labor. Human beings, however, have a unique feature in this respect, for people are ethical beings; they are able to express care and concern for nature, to give expression to their care and its inward ascendant thrust, and to bring degradation and destruction to an end.

The task of social ecology is to study social systems in interaction with ecosystems. Social ecology examines the way in which society is organized. Does society integrate and protect nature, or cause and promote destruction? How do human beings satisfy their needs? Do they do so in solidarity, without creating tension and excluding people, respecting natural cycles and ecological time? How is the earth treated? Is it seen as goods in the marketplace, as a natural resource to exploit, or as a reality to be respected as we respect a part of our body, working with and never against it?

The seriousness of the modern crisis is conditioned by its structural and intrinsic nature. The inadequacy of our treatment of the earth is not something casual and transient; rather, it is the result of a mechanism of accelerated assault, aggression, plunder, and exclusion of nature for the advantage of the present generation. There is a form of socio-economic and political violence directed against peoples, nations, and classes; the consequences are ruined relationships, hunger, disease, and death, and ecological crime against the most complex beings in nature. Violence against nature leads to contamination of the biosphere and degradation of ecosystems. The result now directly affects humankind. The present dominant model of society is a social sin (the rupture of social relations) and an ecological sin (the rupture of relations between humankind and the environment). It is not only present-day classes and ecosystems that are exploited, but future classes and ecosystems. We are all responsible for the mechanisms that comprise a threat of disease and death to social life, in fact to the entire system of planetary life.

In order to stop a tendency that could lead to an ecological apocalypse, it is urgently necessary to introduce processes to assist the development of alternatives to the prevailing social model. Molecular revolutions do occur; that is, revolutions started by social actors who, like molecules, are organized in groups, in a community, in laboratories of thought and action, and in other social movements that have found the courage to live in a new, integrated, and non-fragmented way. Without the courage to take the first few steps, they would be unable to move ahead, and the possibility of a great change would never open up.

The new model of society has to aim at a reconstruction of the social fabric, starting from the multiform potentiality of humankind and society as it is. Not only work but leisure, not only efficiency but gratuitousness, not only productivity but the absurd, playful dimension must be encouraged. Imagination, fantasy, utopia, dreams, emotions, symbolism, poetry, and religion have to be valued as much as production, organization, functionality, and rationality. Masculine and feminine, God and world, body and mind must be integrated on the horizon of a vast cosmic community.

Only thus can society become fully human. Humankind needs both bread and beauty. All that is possible has to be realized, but also a certain amount of the impossible, because human beings are always summoned to try to exceed the limits and to leap over the boundaries established for them. "If we do not attempt the impossible, we shall be forced to face the unacceptable," said the European students in the rebellion year of 1968.

Confronted with an economy of unlimited growth directed toward accumulation, we have to move toward an economy of sufficiency, which focuses on the life of the human person and of nature, the participation of all in the production of the means of living, and solidarity with those persons and those creatures that have lived or suffered through pathological and harsh subsistence conditions. It must also focus on a life that sets great store on tenderness and respect for all creation. Technology should be socially subdivided, so as to produce goods for all and not only for the minority; at the same time it should favor forms of participation and control that avoid all kinds of alienation. This life we lead at present should also be ecologically appropriate, building up the regional ecosystem and guaranteeing the future out of love for the generations to come.

There are some important questions for a social ecology. What kind of education do we need (mental ecology) in order to construct an alliance of sympathy, renewed wonder, and respect for nature? How are we to organize the work system so that it is creative but also joyful? How are we to ensure that our cities are constructed to a human measure in order to promote social virtue and consolidate the bonds of conviviality and communion? What kind of lyricism do we need in order to recover the mystery of the world and to make people sensitive to the interrelationship of all beings? What kind of science should be developed to ensure a fruitful dialogue with the world, without inducing any kind of imbalance? What kind of technology can free people from the enslavement of former historical oppressions (disease, distance, and natural dangers), and also prove spiritually wholesome, helping to restore true equilibrium to the ecosystems of an entire region and create the conditions for a new society? This society will be centered on life and the joy of living, on humanity with its longings, successes, and confusions, and its capacity always to learn from all and everything and, in short, to be able to transcend everything in order to advance toward the great dream of the human heart, which is perfect personal, cosmic and divine integration.

The Ethical Project: Ecoethics

The social dimension takes us to the threshold of ethics, which extends beyond morals. Morality has to do with customs or the knowledge of customs (*mores* = customs = morals). Customs are always circumscribed by the habits, values, and choices within a specific culture and groups that form within it, and by their specific interests, conflicts, and historical privileges. Ethics goes beyond morals to express appropriate behavior and the right way for human beings to relate to one another by respecting the specific and intrinsic dynamics, the essential thrust in the nature of all things. The decisive element in ethics is not that we want it or that we seek to impose it by force (thus creating various different moral standards), but that the same reality states and demands that everyone should heed and be in tune with it. Ethics means an "unlimited responsibility for everything that exists and lives."

The dominant ethics of present-day society is utilitarian and anthropocentric. Humankind believes that everything culminates in the human being. Human beings believe that they are lords and masters of a nature that exists to satisfy their needs and to realize their desires. Basically, as I have observed in the foregoing, this conviction leads to violence and to domination of others and of nature. It denies the subjectivity of other peoples, justice, classes, and the intrinsic value of certain other living creatures in nature. It does not understand that rights do not belong only to humankind and to nations, but also to other beings in creation. There is a human and social right, but there is also an ecological and cosmic right. We do not have the right to what we have not created.

The new ethical order has to find another form of centrality. This should be ecocentric and should seek the equilibrium of the earthly community. Its basic task is to reconstruct the broken alliance between humankind and nature, the alliance between the individual and people, so that henceforth they may be joined in brotherhood and sisterhood, justice and solidarity. The firstfruits of this alliance-making will be peace, which means harmonious movement and full development of life.

Other cultural traditions are important for an ecological ethics. Buddhism and Hinduism in the East, St. Francis of Assisi, Schopenhauer, Albert Schweitzer, and Chico Mendes in the West, developed an ethics of universal compassion, one that seeks harmony, respect, and concern among all creatures, not promoting the advantage of the human race. All that exists deserves to exist and to co-exist peacefully. The essential principle of an ethics of this kind is the following: That is good which conserves and promotes all creatures, especially living creatures, and among living beings, the weakest; that which is bad is everything that prejudices, debases, and destroys living creatures.

The supreme good is to be found in earthly and cosmic integrity. That does not amount merely to the common good of humanity but includes the welfare of nature. Nature is inserted in a universal interwoven complex of relations (the universal energy of microreality and macroreality), and the common good is also necessarily a cosmic affair. We are not confronted merely with the one earth but with the one cosmos with all its bodies, particles, and energies forming a unique interdependent community.

At this level of ethics we become aware of the uniqueness of those particular components of nature known as man and woman. The human being is the sole creature in creation conceived and conceiving itself as an ethical being. This means that only human beings are responsible for making a response (hence responsibility!) to the proposition advanced by creation, for humankind and creation are, in this sense, face to face, in dialogue. This encounter may become one of welcome or of rejection. An alliance may be forged between the partners, and they may become collaborators in a communitarian project of mutual aid and life. Only human beings can assess the pros and cons; study the position from, as it were, without; discern the human situation; and know what legitimate human interests are involved. Only human beings can make sacrifices for the other, out of love; only human beings can, like the Samaritan in the Bible, stoop to aid the weaker party, protecting, supporting, renouncing, and compensating the other. But human beings can also break, destroy, and endanger the whole planetary system. Human beings become an ethical subject in that they can become a subject of history, fulfilling or failing it, for only humankind can produce tragic or fortunate results. The destiny of the whole earth system can depend on the ethical choice made by humanity.

Human beings live ethically when they decide to stop placing themselves above all others and decide instead to stand together with others. To be truly ethical, humankind has to be able to understand the urgent need for ecological balance, of being human together with nature, and of being human together with all other human beings. For the sake of equilibrium human beings must impose limits on their own desires. A human being is not a mere collection of desires. Desire and nothing else makes a person egotistical or a mere imitator of others. Human beings are much more than that, for humans are also creatures of solidarity and communion. Only when people act as responsible administrators, or guardian angels and conservators of creation, will they really live in accordance with the ethical dimension inscribed in their nature.

Then an ecological ethics established on the basis of respect for otherness, on acceptance of diversity, on solidarity, and on the valuation of uniqueness, will help people to dethrone the dominant utilitarian paradigm that is so serious a threat to life and peace among all creatures in nature. This project can take us to a higher level of reflection and commitment.

The Intellectual Project: Mental Ecology

The present situation of the world (atmospheric pollution, soil contamination, the poverty of two-thirds of the human race, and so forth) reveals the state of the human mind or, rather, psyche. We are sick within. Just as there is an external ecology (ecosystems in a state of equilibrium or disequilibrium), so there is an internal ecology. The universe not only exists outside us in its own autonomous state, but also within us. The violence and aggression in the environment grow from roots deep down in the mental structures that have their genealogy and ancestry within us.

All things are within us as images, symbols, and values. Sun, water, plants, and animals live in us as emotional patterns and as archetypes. The positive, traumatic, and inspirational experience that the human psyche has undergone in the course of its long history has been one of contact with nature and also with the body, with the various passions, and with others, men and women, fathers and mothers, aunts and uncles, brothers and sisters, and also strangers. All this has marked the collective unconscious present in each individual. There is a veritable interior archeology in each individual that has been studied by depth psychologists, or Freudian and Jungian psychoanalysts, who have established various codifications that enable them to decipher and read the contents of the psyche.

We know that the process of individuation takes place in a kind of dialogue with the figure and image of the father, mother, family, home, environment, and people and things that are significant for the individual; and we know that this significance can be positive or negative.

Undoubtedly, at a stage when survival was urgent, in an ancestral phase when nature was replete with dangers, human beings were forced to develop their aggressive drive. In more peaceful situations, however, people are free to develop their potential for convivial behavior and reciprocal aid. Behavioral matrices of this kind leave their traces on the internal universe of the human race and on the collective reactions of a nation or people. Another aspect is the process of personal individualization, which recurs in actual forms of behavior. For example, everyone's experience includes an individual ("one's own") world, the body, the family, home, and subjective space. This environment has to be kept in good order. Beyond there is vacuity, amorphous and indeterminate reality, where the garbage of the mind may be thrown and all that one chooses not to preserve may be jettisoned. Or so we think, for we tend to believe that such spaces have no real existence and are uninhabited. The world within also reflects the cultural habit of throwing rubbish into deserted places, lakes, and the sea, which seem to have no owner or guardian.

For the mind of a young child, out of sight is out of mind. An adult, too, may retain the residual notion that an object that he or she does not see no longer exists. Things may lie on the sea bed, or some toxic or nuclear waste may be "discarded" by people who enjoy the wholly illusory feeling that they have actually eliminated it entirely.

The dominant system today, which is the capitalist system, like its recent historical competitor socialism (now in disarray or vanished from vast areas of the world), has developed its own ways of collectively designing and constructing human subjectivity. In reality, systems, including religious and ideological systems, persist only because they succeed in penetrating the human mind, instructing the individual psyche from without. The capitalist and mercantile systems have succeeded in penetrating into every part of the personal and collective human mind. They have managed to decide the individual's way of life, the development of the emotions, the way in which an individual relates to his or her neighbors or strangers, a particular mode of love or friendship, and, indeed, the whole gamut of life and death. These systems lie behind the subjectively induced conviction that life is meaningless if it lacks symbols of power and status, such as a respectable level of consumption and the ownership of specific electrical goods, machines, art objects, homes, and other symbols of prestige.

Systems control human life, and any attempt to create an alternative way of living is made extremely difficult or hazardous by this determinative power of the dominant ethos. Marcuse was right when he wrote of the one-dimensional human being as characteristic of the modern era. Society represses the natural needs and impulses of human beings, whom it controls by misrepresenting real needs and by manipulating false needs, which the system creates to serve its vested interests. Sexuality, for instance, is projected as the mere discharge of emotional tension in the course of an exchange process between two sets of genital organs. The true nature of sexuality is denied, for sex is not something found merely in the bedroom, but extends over the whole of human existence, with its potential tenderness, the possibility of true encounter, and the capacity to eroticize male-female relations.

The human needs associated with possession and survival are similarly distorted and manipulated. The instinct of ownership is exaggerated and wrongly emphasized so that the accumulation of material goods becomes a virtue, and work is presented only as the production of wealth. In the technological age our psyches are invaded by inanimate objects without any human reference. These objects create loneliness. The information obtained from databases and structured or manipulated by computers is deprived of real affective components.

A form of individualism has been developed that is proper to an arid personality, with fragmented emotions and hostile and antisocial attitudes. Other people are seen as strangers and hostages to the fortune or satisfaction of the individual and his or her needs. There is a tendency to conceal the other basic necessity of human beings, which is the need to be, to develop one's own individual identity.

This self-creation has nothing to do with the collective manipulation and manufacture of subjectivity, but with freedom, creativity, courage, and the readiness to venture onto difficult and more personal pathways of choice and achievement. This dimension is subversive as far as the dominant social suasions are concerned. Only by starting from authentic social, moral, and religious premises can the human individual sensibly confront the world of possession and empty desire without succumbing to its imperatives and falling victim to its fetishism. A Native American has said: "When the last tree has been felled, and when the last river has been seized, only then will we finally realize that we cannot eat money."

Mental ecology tries to recover the original state of maimed human intimacy, and to value and love nature. It tries to develop the human capacity for celebration and conviviality, and to stress the news that all human beings bear in their very presence, in their relations to the whole environment, with all the potentiality of emotions suffused with wonder at the universe contemplated in all its complexity, majesty, and grandeur. Mental ecology tries to recharge the positive psychic energy of the human being needed to confront the onerous challenge of existence and the contradictions of our dualistic, macho, and consumerist culture. Mental ecology promotes the development of the magical and shamanistic dimension of our minds. We know that each of us has the potential not only to summon and use reasoning power but to tune into those forces in the universe that can become manifest in us by way of our drives, visionary impulses, intuitions, dreams, and creativity. Every human being is creative by nature. Even when we copy or imitate others, following their blueprints, we do so in our own unique and inimitable way.

In these ways the human being can open himself or herself up to the original cosmic dynamism that enables everyone to realize his or her own variety and reach ever new levels of individual complexity, and thus ever higher levels of reality and life.

Without a revolution of the mind, it will not be possible to bring about a revolution in relations between humankind and nature. The new alliance has its roots in the depths of the human being. There humankind must work out the great and splendid motives and the secret magic that transforms the appearance of all reality, so that it assumes its rightful place as a link in the vast communitarian chain of the cosmos.

The Spiritual Project: Cosmic Mysticism

Ethics degenerates into codified precepts and rote behavior, and mental ecology runs the risk of disappearing in its extraordinary inward world, if neither expresses a form of spirituality or mysticism. When we speak of mysticism, we think of a fundamental and all-inclusive experience, by means of which we embrace the totality of things, an organic totality as it were, replete with meaning and value. Mysticism is connected to spirituality. A spirit, in its original sense, from which the term spirituality is derived, is every being that draws breath; hence spirit refers to all living beings, such as human beings, animals, and plants. But that is not all. The whole earth and the universe are experienced as bearers of spirit, because they are sources of life and furnish all the elements that are needed for life, yet also sustain the thrust of creation.

Spirituality is that attitude which puts life at the center, and defends and promotes life against all the mechanisms of death, desiccation, or stagnation. The opposite of spirit, in this sense, is not the body but death and everything associated with the system of death, understood in the widest sense of biological, social, and existential death (failure, humiliation, and oppression). Nourishing spirituality means cultivating that inward space, the basis of which all things can be brought together. It means overcoming deadness and stagnation and living reality in terms of values, inspiration, and symbols of higher meaning. The spiritual person is one who is always in a position to see the other side of reality, and who is always capable of perceiving that profundity by which we are referred to the Ultimate Reality that religions call God.

Spirituality does not start from power, or from the accumulative instinct, or from instrumental reason. It relies on the movements of sacramental and symbolic reason, on the gratuitousness of the world, on relationships, on deep stirrings within, on the sense of communion that all things possess, and on a vision of the vast cosmic organism, shot through and permeated with signs of and allusions to a higher and fuller reality.

In this modern age we arrive at that level only by way of a strict critique of the paradigm of modernity, of the kind I have tried to sketch in these pages. We have to take this understanding forward and incorporate it in an even greater global awareness. The ecological crisis reveals the crisis of profound meaning in our way and system of life, and in our model of society and development.

We can no longer base ourselves on power in the sense of domination, and on the irresponsible greed of nations and of individuals. We can no longer pretend to stand as gods above all other aspects of the universe; we must advance hand in hand with life itself and promote what is truly living. Development has to support nature and must relinquish any stance contrary to nature. Today we can no longer engage in a worldwide promotion of the interests of capital, commerce, science, and technology. Instead we must promote solidarity with all living beings, starting with the least favored, a passionate valuation of life in all its forms, participation as a response to the appeals of all human beings and to the thrust of the universe, and respect for nature, for which we are all responsible. On such a basis we can and should assimilate science and technology as ways of helping us to guarantee, preserve, and/or reconstruct ecological equilibrium, and to ensure an equable satisfaction of our needs in an adequate and not unconsciously wasteful manner.

The master spirits of the modern ethos of relations between people and nature have strayed from this admirable path. Descartes in his theory of knowledge (his "Discourse on Method") maintains that the human vocation consists in being "masters and proprietors of nature." Another of the founding fathers of the modern attitude, Bacon, expresses the meaning of knowledge in these dubious terms: "Knowledge is power." Power over nature, according to Bacon, is a prime necessity: "Now we govern nature in opinions, but we are thrall to her in necessity; but if we would be led by her invention, we should command her by action" (*In Praise of Human Knowledge*).

Instead, we should go back to those old masters who established a very different spiritual tradition, one more concerned with integration, and who inaugurated a new kind of tenderness in the face of nature, following the examples of Francis of Assisi, Teilhard de Chardin and the entire great Augustinian, Bonaventuran, Pascalian, and existentialist tradition. None of these masters believed that knowledge was a form of appropriation and of domination of things, but rather a form of love and of communion with things. They valued emotion as a way of communicating with the world and as a way of experiencing the divine. Pascal rightly said that faith meant perceiving God with the heart and not the reason.

Today, ecological concern and especially the current cosmological understanding of the world rely on this spirituality of integration. A spiritual revolution is taking place which demands a truly sensitive and serious apprehension of the problems that actually confront us in life.

Let us examine some of the findings of science that make it all the more urgent to ensure that this particular revolution succeeds.

According to quantum physics and the theory of relativity, matter and energy are interchangeable and equivalent. Indeed, atomic physics no longer recognizes the concept of matter. Within the atom there is a vast empty space. Elementary particles are no more than energy at a high level of concentration and stability. Matter does not exist other than as a tendency or notion. Basically, Einstein's formula means that matter and energy are but two aspects of one and the same reality.

The subatomic particles, in their turn, appear as electromagnetic waves or as particles, depending on the viewpoint of the observer. Consequently, the field of application and validity of linear logic and of the principle of non-contradiction is somewhat restricted. Factor A may be A but equally non-A. Niels Bohr has introduced the complementarity principle, which is very much in accordance with Chinese philosophy, according to which reality is organized as yin and yang (matter/spirit, feminine/masculine, negative/positive, and so on).

Werner Heisenberg formulated the principle of indeterminacy, according to which atomic particles do not obey causal logic but are organized in accordance with the principle of the indeterminate nature of probability. Probability is no longer probability but becomes reality depending on the presence of an observer who may be a human being or some other element of nature that establishes a relationship. Probability as such is not open to description. The act of observation changes the function of probability in a discontinuous way. The transition from the possible to the real takes place during the act of observation, says Heisenberg.

This viewpoint acknowledges that the observing subject influences the phenomenon observed. Moreover, the observer, according to quantum physics, is indispensable to the constitution and to the observation of the characteristics of an atomic phenomenon. The subject is part of reality as conceived and described. Reality is to be described as the subject describes it. The human being is a constitutive part of everything, and human consciousness necessarily defines that part of reality which is under observation.

The new physics introduces the concept of the world as a unified and inseparable whole. The universe consists of a highly complex network of relationships in all directions and in all forms. Hence the laws of physics are merely statistical in nature. Causality, moreover, is non-linear. Reality A influences B, which in its turn reinfluences A and also C, and so forth.

In this understanding, everything is dynamic. Everything vibrates. Everything is in process in a permanent dance of energy and elements.

According to holographic theory (holography is a kind of reconstruction and photography of waves, in which lasers produce the "images" as "holograms"), the parts are in the whole and the whole in every part. A Nobel prizewinner for physics, David Bohm, starting from this principle, suggests an image of universal order as a development in spiral form. Everything implies everything, nothing exists outside a relational situation, and relationship constitutes reality as a whole and altogether. What exists is "holomovement," a form of movement articulated in all directions and uniting all parts. Every one of us is included in every part and in the whole of the universe. We constitute a unique universe in which everything is connected with everything else.

While physics offers a new understanding of the material world, contemporary biology offers us new perspectives on life. The combination of quantum physics and biology has transformed our understanding of the nature of the systems of living organisms and of the cosmos itself. It has also helped us to understand nature more proficiently as an organic whole. I shall mention only a few points here.

Non-linearity: At a deep level there is no such thing as a cause and effect relationship, but instead a simultaneous and permanent fabric of global relations.

Dynamics: All parts of a system are in perpetual motion. The organism does not derive its stability from fixed laws, but from its capacity to adapt and from its dynamic equilibrium.

The cyclic character of growth: Growth is non-linear. Decay and death form part of life. Death is an invention of life. The cycle promotes the continuation of life, not the perpetuation of the individual. Nature is not biocentric but ecocentric, because it is related to the equilibrium between life and death in a perspective of universal maintenance.

The structural order of things: Every system consists of subsystems, and they all form part of an even greater system. The human being is part of the system of humanity. Humanity is part of the animal system, which in its turn is part of the vegetable system and, in the end, of the earth organism.

Autonomy and integration: Every system is autonomous and exists in its own relational time, enjoying its own identity but remaining open so as always to be included in a process of integration with all elements of the environment. Darwin spoke of the struggle for life as the principle of natural selection. The fittest survive; the principle of self-affirmation triumphs. But now we can improve on Darwin's finding with the observation that the principle that guarantees survival is one of integration, cooperation, exchange, and symbiosis. We must stress not merely difference and identity but complementarity and solidarity.

Self-organization and creativity: Every complex system, such as the central nervous system, has the property of self-organization. There is a continuous process of learning and selection under way. Creativity is intrinsic to living creatures, and evolution is always intent on promoting the creative capacity. The human being is a creative being par excellence.

It should be clear why certain ecologists understand the earth as a single complex system, as a living organism: Gaia. Every subsystem is linked to all other subsystems through the blowing of the winds, the oceans, the migration of species, the cycles of growth, maturation, aging and death. By means of the air that we breathe we are united with all animals, all plants, but also our vehicles, factories, and all our industrial chimneys.

In addition to these findings of physics and biology, we have the suggestions of depth psychology, transpersonal psychology, and the so-called new anthropology. It is not possible to describe all these contributions in detail. However, they all

agree on the fact that the human being, biologically and men-
tally (psychologically), has an ancestral past, just as the universe may be said to have one. There is an inward ecology that
is connected with all the energy of the cosmos passing through
us, so that we are linked to the destiny of all creatures. As
American ecologist Thomas Berry says, the human being is
more than a creature living on the earth and in the universe,
for a human being is above all a dimension of the earth and of
the universe. The formation of our way of being depends on
the maintenance and on the orientation of this universal order.
Every creature in the universe is, as it were, preoccupied by
us. There is a benign conspiracy among all living beings
(Ferguson). We cannot separate waves from one another or from
the sea. We cannot separate light from the shining of that light
and from its irradiation. Everything co-exists.

Spirituality and science are complementary. As we learn
more about contemporary cosmology, we discover that the
planet is a vast complex organism. When one part of that organism is violated, we suffer too. Science is not the only way
of knowing, for we also apprehend things proficiently through
our conscience, our inwardness, our intuitions, our dreams, and
our predictive imaginings.

Great scientists are ecstatic when they come face to face
with the complexity of reality and confront the Force behind
cosmic energy. This entire vast organism does in fact possess
a unifying Principle. A profound form of spirituality can develop without necessarily leading to any specific confession.
This is not so much a matter of adhering to a religious faith as
of professing a cosmic spirituality, like Albert Einstein.

The dynamic principle of the self-determination of the universe is at work in every part and in the whole without name
or image. Nevertheless, God is the name that religions use to
avoid anonymity and to touch our awareness and our celebration of life. God is the name for mystery, an expression of our
respect. God is at the center of the universe. Humankind feels
integrated in God, in a humble supporting role; integrated to-

gether with all other creatures, but at the same time responsible and co-creative, sons and daughters of the Supreme Lord, who always becomes a beggar in order to be close to everyone.

We want not only to know, but to experience God. There is nothing more appropriate to an ecological mentality than to realize that Mystery is involved in everything, penetrates everything, shines in everything, and sustains everything. There is no one way and no one door leading to God. That is a Western illusion, especially of the Christian church. So that we may one day experience the Mystery that we call God, everything is a way and all living creatures are sacraments and gates to a meeting with God.

Ecology and Theology: Christian Panentheism

The ecological challenge also confronts theology. Doing theology always means asking what connection there is between this situation and God. Theology has to review past conceptions, see if others are needed, and in the light of new problems, update old ways of looking at things that fit only the experience of the past and not the major questions of the moment.

Christianity's Co-responsibility for the Ecological Crisis

Self-criticism comes first. Is Christianity co-responsible for the present ecological crisis? Yes, it is. It has had a decisive influence, in the West at least.

We know that the book of origins (Genesis) presents two versions of creation and of the mission of humankind. The first version says: "Let us make man [man and woman] in our image, after our likeness; and let them have dominion. . . . Be fruitful and multiply, and fill the earth and subdue it; and have dominion over the fish of the sea. . . . " (Gen 1:26,28). On the one hand, there is the significance of the text in the cultural environment of the hagiographer of some three thousand years ago, and on the other hand there is the question of the reception of this text by readers today in a different cultural environment. The original meaning of the text is this: The human being, man or woman, is a representative of God in creation, his son or daughter, helping to carry out God's creative work. God makes the human being a creator. That is the exegetical significance of the reference to "image and likeness." The terms "dominion" and "subdue" are to be understood in this context and not in any despotic sense, as the words might suggest. The son and daughter of God (the other meaning of "image and likeness") share in the nature of the Father-creator, which is wisdom and goodness. Their mission does not culminate in creative work, in mere responsible representation of God, but in rest on the sabbath, which is celebration made actual in terms of the perfection and goodness of all creation (Gen 2:2-3). At the summit of the human mission we find, not work, but leisure, not struggle but gratuitousness and joyful rest.

But that is not the meaning that has prevailed. The words "dominion" and "subdue" are not reinterpreted in the context of the modern world but are taken literally. The human mission is still conceived in the way that Descartes and Bacon expressed most acutely: the human being is intended to dominate and harness the forces of nature for the individual and social welfare of humanity. This interpretation, apparently supported by God's powerful word, legitimizes the ravages the earth has had to undergo and still suffers. We have to revise this conception and to recover the original and profoundly ecological meaning of the biblical message.

The second version says that the human being was made by God as a living being, that God "breathed into his nostrils the breath of life." He was placed in the garden of Eden "to till it and keep it" (Gen 2:15). The meaning is clear. The human being is a friend of nature, works with the earth (which he or she is to till), and acts as the good angel of the earth, in order to safeguard it. This meaning should have qualified the first but in fact was obscured or spiritualized. The context of our Western culture ordained an orientation to power and pharaonism. Today, in a context of crisis for our paradigm of society, the original message is increasingly important. A responsible and effective ecological policy accords with the faith of the Bible.

Beyond these texts, a certain theological tradition dominant in some ecclesiastical circles encouraged suspicion of physicality, disdain for the world, rejection of all forms of pleasure, and contempt for sexuality and femininity. It favored the idea of a God detached from the world, thus promoting the formation of a world separate from God. All such tendencies assist in the abandonment of the world to human aggressivity.

But certain positive elements act as a counterbalance to these negative trends: the affirmation of matter by virtue of the mystery of the incarnation; the sacraments, especially the sacrament of the eucharist; the resurrection as a transfiguration of the world, of matter, and of the human body; the discovery of the sacramental nature of the cosmos, receiving the very blessing of God; the mystery of creation, which makes all living creatures brothers and sisters; and the mysticism of brotherhood and sisterhood of St. Francis, St. Clare, and their followers.

The Liberation of Creation Theology

More than any other science, ecology confronts nature as an organic, differentiated, and single whole. This helps us to understand the theological notion of creation, according to which God and the universe differ from one another and at the same time are like one another. To say that we are created means affirming that we have come from God, that we bear in ourselves the marks of God, and that we are travelling toward God. The dominant trend of Christian reflection has not taken the mystery of creation to any very profound level of consideration. For historical and institutional reasons, there has been much more concentration on the mystery of redemption. But there has always been a current of thought that has attempted a more appropriate articulation of creation and redemption in a line of thought handed down from St. Francis, and taken to greater speculative depths by St. Bonaventure, Duns Scotus, and William of Ockham; viz. the modern theology of earthly reality (of the world, politics, and liberation) and the entire theology of the Orthodox church.

Above all, we should see the creation as the expression of God's joy, as the dance of God's love, as the mirror of both God and all created things. In this sense every creature is a messenger of God, and God's representative as well as sacrament. Everyone is worthy and is to be accepted and listened to as such.

In this vision, which places such an emphasis on creation, there is no form of hierarchy and no exclusive representative of any kind. Everyone derives from the same love of God. Revelation is permanent, in continuous process, for God continues to give the divine self and to ensure the historical appearance of other dimensions of this divine mystery with the development of the same creation. The cosmic magisterium offers us infallible instruction on the humility, tenderness, and goodness of the all-sustaining principle, God.

In this theology of creation we can discern the special place accorded to humankind. The human being is not to be found at the top but behind and at the end of creation. The human being is the last to appear and is found behind, as it were, the front lines. The world is not the product of human desire or human creativity. Humanity did not see the beginning. Being antecedent to humankind, the world does not belong to humanity. It belongs to God, its creator. But the world is assigned to humanity to till and keep. Therefore the relationship the human being enjoys with the creation is essentially one of responsibility; it is an ethical relationship. This responsibility is not, however, the result of a human freedom that can decide to gratify itself with the world. The responsibility is anterior to that freedom and is inscribed in its creational liberty. Freedom is realized within the world that human beings have not created, but in which they are located.

Human beings are made in such a way that they always find themselves with and in the creation, proceeding in accordance with the divine thrust which they bear, having received it from God, in whose image and likeness humankind is made. In other words, human beings can be human and fulfilled only by fulfilling the world and by insertion in that world, by laboring in it and caring for it. But humankind, in tilling and keeping the earth, is neither destructive nor dominant. We have a commitment that is profoundly ecological and intended to maintain the equilibrium of the creation, which progresses and is transformed by virtue of human labor.

A theology of creation helps us to understand the meaning of a theology of redemption. Redemption presupposes a drama, a degeneration of creation, a failure of human vocation that has affected all human beings and their cosmic environment. Humankind bears a retributive wound for not having tilled and kept the creation. Therefore, as St. Paul says, humankind suffers and groans as it longs for freedom from its yoke (Rom 8:22).

Redemption implies not a replacement but a recovery. Essentially, the creation has kept its status as a good creation. Humankind does not have absolute power over God's work to the point of doing it absolute and essential harm, but can injure it seriously. Otherwise we could not speak of redemption but only of substitution, of the creation of another nature. Redemption as it were picks up creation, resets the hands, and staunches the bleeding wounds. This means that biblical revelation, the church, the magisterium, and the sacraments possess a relative status. They always exist in relation to the creation and serve its recovery. That is not always stated. When we forget creation, we tend to exaggerate the importance of the Bible (fundamentalism), inflate the role of the church (ecclesiocentrism), and exaggerate the function of the sacraments (sacramentalism). The Hebrew and Christian revelation is intended to recover and not to replace the revelation of creation. This does not mean that we should denigrate the Bible as against science, or make a fetish of the ecclesiastical magisterium, as if it had access to a secret form of knowledge that others are denied and that lies behind creation and is known by means of various forms of knowledge.

The ecclesial community must feel part of the human community, and the human community has to feel that it is part of the cosmic community. They all form part of the trinitarian community of Father, Son, and Holy Spirit.

The Trinity Is Interactive: An Ecological God

Ecology is a complex and complete interplay of relations. It includes everything, disregards nothing, values everything, and cares for everything. It relies on the foremost intuition of Christianity: its divine conception. It affirms the one nature of the Godhead, but at the same time maintains the diversity of the divine Persons without in any way "multiplying" God as a number of gods. Christianity has always believed that God is Father, Son, and Holy Spirit. These divine Persons co-exist eternally, distinct, united, equally eternal and infinite. They are simultaneously, and there is no precedence among them, no subordination, and no sequence.

We are not concerned with any image of three gods, which is only a soft version of many gods. The Trinity is three distinct Persons, but the links of life, the loving correlations, and the eternal interplay of relations among them is such that the three exist, subsist, in one. They are the one God-communion, the one God-relation, the one God-love.

The universe is a reproduction of this diversity and of this union. The world, indeed, is complex, diverse, one, united, interrelated, because it is a reflection of the Trinity. God invades every being, enters into every relationship, erupts into every ecosystem. But God especially sacramentalizes the life of every human individual, because there we find intelligence, will, and sensibility as distinct concretizations of our one humanity, whole and entire. We are a unique life and form of communion realized distinctly. We are one and at the same time multiple, like the mystery of the triune God.

The Holy Spirit Dwells in the Cosmos and in the Human Heart

The foregoing reflections have shown that our cosmos consists of energy in a permanently interactive state, which assumes forms of greater density in the shape of various life-systems. There is good reason, with some thinkers, to believe that everything is a manifestation of life, because life is self-interactive energy at the highest level of complexity.

This life takes a thousand concrete forms, from the primitive movement of the original matter/energy, to its self-conscious expression in human beings.

Christian tradition possesses a category which it uses to express reality as energy and life. This is the image of the Holy Spirit, who is the Creator Spirit par excellence. The Spirit acts in and moves through all things, lord and giver of life. The Spirit sustains the prophets, inspires poets, fires charismatic impulses, and fills the hearts of all men and women with enthusiasm.

The Spirit, according to scripture, fills the universe to its limits, and constantly renews the structure of the cosmos. The Spirit dwells in creation in the same way as the Son, who is incarnate in the humanity of Jesus.

Christians do not find it difficult to understand the idea of the incarnation, in which the Son of God became human and cohabited with our dramatic human destiny. We also believe in the cosmic presence of the risen Christ, who is active in the process of evolution, as Teilhard affirmed so brilliantly in his work on the cosmic Christ, yet we do scant justice to the reality of the Spirit's indwelling in creation. The Spirit has made the cosmos a temple, the scene of the Spirit's action and manifestation.

Christians can develop various attitudes to the biotic and abiotic created universe. They may develop a spontaneous cosmic spirituality linked to the processes of nature and history. Women are much more adept at integration, for women are much closer than men to the mystery of life. It was not without reason that Mary, the Mother of God, entered into a unique relationship with the Spirit, who "came upon her" and whose power "overshadowed" her (Lk 1:35), thus divinizing the feminine for all time.

A poet of long ago who experienced this mysticism of the ubiquitous Spirit put it very well when he wrote that the Spirit sleeps in stone, dreams in flowers, awakens in animals, knows he is awake in men, and feels awake in women. This is a sympathetic intuition of the cosmic ubiquity of the Spirit, as testified to by so many mystics of various cultures, such as the Sioux Indians of North America, the Bororos of Brazil, and a number of Eastern Zen masters. The Fathers of the Latin and Greek church of the fourth and fifth centuries, especially Gregory of Nazianzus and Gregory of Nyssa, St. Basil and St. Peter Damian, express in various ways the *Spiritus ubique diffusus* (the universally diffused Spirit).

Such visions can sustain an ecological mysticism. We are immersed in a sea of life, spirit, sensation and communion. We form a whole in the Spirit who, like the thread of a pearl necklace, unites each and all as they mount toward the highest point of communion in the fullness and kingdom of the Trinity.

Christian Pan-en-theism: Everything in God, God in Everything

A particularly appropriate idea for the cosmic ubiquity of the Spirit is panentheism. This is a very old and noble Christian concept that can strengthen our spirituality and enrich our theological understanding of ecology. First of all, naturally, we must remember that panentheism is quite different from pantheism. Pantheism maintains that everything is God, and that primordial energy, atoms, stones, mountains, stars, and human beings form part of the deity. Then things, living beings, and persons are but different manifestations of the same unique substantial reality, which is God. According to pantheism, things are not things in themselves, possessing autonomy, but concretizations and synonyms of the same reality, that is, the cosmic and universal God.

Panentheism, however, starts from the distinction between God and the creature, yet always maintains the relation between them. The one is not the other. Each of them has his/her/its own relative autonomy yet is always related. Not everything is God, but God is in everything, as we might deduce from the etymology of the word pantheism. God flows through all things; God is present in everything and makes of all reality a temple. And then, vice versa, everything is in God. We are only through God, we move only through God, because we are always in God, for indeed: "It is in him that we live and move and have our being" (Acts 17:28).

Panentheism is a most appropriate way of embracing and encompassing the universe, for it means that we are always in a state of approaching one and the same trinitarian God. This experience gives rise to a new integrative and holistic spirituality that can unite heaven and earth. Albert Einstein said that he believed that the cosmic religious feeling was the strongest and highest motive of scientific research. It is indeed the motive not only of research but of an open existence, without physical dread or material fear, an existence of ultra-solidity or ultra-refulgence. The world is not only a bridge to God. It is also the place where God is honored and worshiped, and the place where we meet God. This truth enables us to understand what the greatest Western mystic Meister Eckhart meant when he said that if the soul could know God without the world, the world would never have been created. We and the world exist so that we may accept the invitation to share in God's superabundance and accompany God in the divine venture undertaken within our humanity and createdness.

The Western Archetype of Ecological Thinking: Francis of Assisi

Essentially, ideas are true only when they take concrete, biographical form in individuals and in historical movements. Western culture includes a figure who became the archetype of an exemplary form of brotherhood and sisterhood with nature: Francis of Assisi. Accordingly, he has been called the patron saint of ecology.

The originality of St. Francis is to be found in the successful and happy synthesis he established between internal and external ecology: he produced an outstanding form of cosmic mysticism. Contemporary biographers, Thomas of Celano, St. Bonaventure, and witnesses who were in fact associates of Francis (*Legend of Three Companions*, *Perugian Legend*, and *Sacrum Commercium*), unanimously confirmed the profound empathy he felt with and for all creatures. Francis was a brilliant poet, capable of reaching into the heart of things, of deciphering the ontological message, and of sensing by connatural sympathy the bond that unites each one to all others and to the Father's heart. He perceived not only the mystical meaning of divine sonhood and daughterhood, of what is known as filiation, but the explicit, concrete manifestations of that theological truth. We are sons and daughters, and therefore we are brothers and sisters. He used the loving terms brother and sister to address the moon, fire and water, and even weeds, sickness, and death.

On the basis of this mysticism of universal brotherhood and sisterhood, Francis treated all things with great respect and tenderness. He told his associates not to cut the trees down completely, so that they could grow again, and not to take all the bees' honey, lest they starve. Tender and loving concern was his fundamental attitude to all that was other than himself. *Eros* and *pathos* (the capacity to feel and to pulsate with care for the value of people and things) predominated in him over the *logos* (the structure of understanding reality). With Francis the heart came into its own once again as an acute and profound way of knowing. The knowledge of the heart was not estranged from reality but instead reinforced communion and friendship with actuality. This constituted the outward ecology of St. Francis.

But Francis also developed an entire inward ecology (mental ecology). In his writings, in his prayers, and in his songs, we feel the lively enthusiasm the universe induced in his experience of the world and of God. At the end of his life he composed a hymn to his brother the sun, which is replete with the highest degree of cosmic ecstasy. He wrote it when he was almost entirely blind and very sick. He hymned the sun and the moon, the wind and water, fire and earth, elements he did not see with his almost completely exhausted eyes, but which were present to him inwardly and intimately as perfectly integrated symbols and archetypes. His hymn celebrated the cosmic marriage of heaven and earth, and of human existence with all things and with the solar God who shone in the depths of his heart. The philosopher Paul Ricoeur put it very well when he said that he both self-expressed and expressed the world and explored his own holiness when he tried to understand and explain the world. St. Francis offers a vast testimony to this ecological truth.

The West has never seen such loving kindness and tenderness, as a form of life and integration, as in Francis of Assisi. Therefore he continues to act as a cultural reference point for everyone who tries to establish a new alliance with creation. Dante called him the "sun of Assisi" that continues to shine throughout our own times, awakening in us the power and inclination to become more aware of, allied to, and compassionate toward all beings in the cosmos.

St. Francis also shows us that the option for the poor and the most impoverished of all (lepers and AIDS victims), the option which the Poverello himself made, accords with tender love for the creation. That was the love that took him to the lepers and to the wolf of Gubbio, which made him embrace beggars and speak to the birds. He knew that this world was subject to the rule of inequality (*regio dissimilitudinis*), but he did not interpret that as meaning that life should be governed by bitterness and rancor. Unlimited poetry, song, dancing, and love are able to transform things. A joyous and rejoicing God is before all else the liberator of the poor.

With St. Francis we recover the conviction that paradise is not lost to all people and things, and that we can return to carry out the divine vocation testified to in Genesis. Our very own place is indeed the earth, our mother and friend, but in its due state as the garden of Eden, ours to cultivate with loving care and to guard with all the tender force that we can summon from our hearts.

CHAPTER 2

Religion, Social Justice, and a New Appeal of Creation

An unmistakable phenomenon is universally observable to-day: the return of religious and mystical feeling. This is not a reaffirmation of the permanence of the historical religions that have resisted all kinds of attacks, aggressions, and persecutions by political forces, and even attempts on the part of critical and scientific thought to undermine their claims to legitimacy. The novelty is to be found in the revelation that the very heirs of critical and scientific knowledge are becoming religious and mystical.

It is important to understand the relevance of this fact and to draw whatever lesson it has for us, as well as to know its function in the larger process in which we are all involved because of the cultural transformation now under way. First, I shall examine the form taken by this return of the mystical and religious dimension.

Religion: Deviation or the Right Way?

One characteristic of the modern era is the central position of reason in the understanding of life and in the organization of life and of human society. Science and technology are more complete expressions of this same form of rationalism. It is responsible for the growth of the biggest rationalist myth, which is the myth of unlimited growth. In its name the earth has been given a new look, and a vast number of nations and social groups have achieved a certain material well-being. Nevertheless, a high social price has been paid for this unlimited linear development. Immense numbers of human beings have been sacrificed to progress, or have benefited only in a secondary or marginal way. Nature has suffered a destructive onslaught. In some areas the destruction has had irreversible effects.

The first stage of the scientific-technological project seemed wholly engaging and fascinating. In fact, it amounted to the creation of portentous works. Then came wars in which science and technology revealed their unimaginable capacity for destruction. Nuclear, chemical, and biological weapons have made an apocalypse for all nature a possibility. From admiration and wonder we have moved to fear and then to terror. We run the risk of producing viruses that will resist any antibiotic. In this way we threaten the whole biosphere and compromise the very survival of humanity itself. Science can cease to act as a creative demiurge and become instead a destructive demon. This awareness has created an urgent need and demand for ethics, arising from our consciousness of our responsibility for the future of the earth. There has also been strong criticism of the rational paradigm of humanity. The myth of unlimited development could lead to destruction. We have to find alternatives to modernity. We cannot abandon reason, because we need it to administer the complex human project and also to correct the harm done by the products of reason. We have to overcome rationalism-cum-reason (conceived of as the sole legitimate form of access to and dominion of reality), and to integrate reason in a greater whole.

How has modernity seen religion? Mainly as something premodern. According to modern thought, religion reproduces a primitive form of knowledge that has to be replaced by critical and scientific thought (Comte). Consequently, religion is viewed as weak and as opium, alienation, and false consciousness of what has not yet been discovered, and of what has just been lost (Marx), and also as the illusions of a neurotic mind trying to satisfy the desire for protection and to make fear tolerable (Freud). In short, religion is seen as a reality that (in spite of its capacity to transform society) tends to ignore the process of rationalization, secularization, and disenchantment of the world (Weber). Others have seen it as meaningless, because religious discourse has no verifiable object (the Vienna School; Popper and Carnap).

Religion is distinct from reason. It is located in the realms of imagination, feeling, and desire, factors that interfere with the rational pursuit of objectivity.

Nevertheless philosopher, mathematician, and finally mystic Ludwig Wittgenstein remarked that the human being amounts to more than the rational and scientific attitude that is always concerned to investigate how things are and to seek an answer to everything. There is also the human capability of rapture or wonder. "Wonder cannot be expressed in a question. Consequently there is no answer" (*Schriften*, 3.68). The fact that the world exists is wholly inexpressible. "There are, indeed, things that cannot be put into words. They *make themselves manifest*. They are what is mystical" (*Tractatus*, 6.522). "It is not *how* things are in the world that is mystical, but *that* it exists" (*Tractatus*, 6.44). "We feel that even when all *possible* scientific questions have been answered, the problems of life remain completely untouched. Of course there are then no questions left, and this itself is the answer" (*Tractatus*, 6.52). To believe in God is to grasp the problem of the meaning of life. To believe in God means affirming that life has meaning. We cannot speak of God in the same way that we cannot speak of this world. "What we cannot speak about we must pass over in silence" (*Tractatus,* 7). The limits of the scientific spirit are to be found where there is that which we must pass over in silence.

Reasoning begins with reason. Reason itself is not a factor of reason. Long ago the ancient wisdom of the Upanishads put it thus: "That by which all thinking thinks cannot itself be thought." Perhaps we cannot explicate religion at all.

But wonder, the sublime, and that presence that is being in its most open manifestation do exist. A contemporary Jewish thinker has written: "Shut up in our studies, we are removed from all other considerations when this or that idea suddenly enters our mind. Then and there it may seem reasonable to say that the world is worthless and that everything is a dream or fiction. But even then no one can regard the stars with disgust, ignore the dawn, scorn the flowering of spring, or hold cheap the complexity of being. Far from the immensity of everything, imprisoned in our own vanities, we can disdain and adversely criticize everything. But between heaven and earth we are rendered speechless" (A. Heschel, *God in Search of Man*).

Religion is not what human beings do when they are alone, but that which human beings do in the presence of what makes them wonder, that which fills their heart, and that which makes them feel it is beyond all reason. Surely it is in such circumstances that it is meaningful to speak of God? In fact, it is in precisely such a context that all religions do speak of God as a presence: the presence of the sublime, of the luminous, of ultimate receptivity, of the sacred, and of ultimate meaning.

Today we are experiencing a new perception of this presence of God. The hidden roots of the recovery of the religious and mystical dimension are not absolutely but only in one sense to be found in the crisis of the paradigm of modernity, which is knowledge: the knowledge of domination; domination for the sake of wealth; wealth by exploitation. That paradigm acts like a veil that prevents us from discerning God's presence. Without that impediment, the eyes see what is present, the gratuitous advent of the divine and the possibility of human rapture. This perception underlies all healthy religiousness. It is that which reflects the undaunted return of the religious and mystical dimension in all world cultures, and a new capacity for wonder, admiration, and magic.

People want to experience God. They are tired of being cat-echized, of listening to religious authority speak about God, and of theologians proffering traditional doctrine in mere up-dated language. The words of Job are relevant to the present situation: "Who is this that hides counsel without knowledge? Therefore I have uttered what I did not understand, things too wonderful for me, which I did not know. 'Hear, and I will speak; I will question you, and you declare to me.' I had heard of thee by the hearing of the ear, but now my eye sees thee" (Job 42:3-5).

The recovery of the religious and mystical dimension does not generally occur through religious institutions. They speak of God and of miracles but find it difficult to agree to expe-rience God and to live God's breaking forth in life. They find it difficult to do what is needed: to seek personal and communitarian experience of a new immersion in the utterly absorbing mystery of God, present in history and in the trans-formation of life.

This phenomenon makes us ask, What is the point of reli-gion? Where does religious and mystical experience come from? This can be answered directly: in the instances condemned by modern reason, in fantasy, in the realm of the imagination, and in the depths of desire where free rein is given to all the dreams and utopias that fill the mind, enthusing human hearts and light-ing the fuse for the breakthrough to the transformation of his-tory. To cite Blaise Pascal, religious experience is derived from instinct and feeling, but above all from the movement of the heart and not from the spirit of geometry, for "it is the heart that sees God and not the reason."

These instances, desire, fantasy, and imagination, do not adapt to the concrete facts, to things as they are, but contest them, suspecting what is indeed true—that the real is much more than the apparently given. We apprehend the potentiality in actuality, sensing what is not yet but could be. Utopia does not conflict with reality. Utopia discloses the potential and ideal dimension of reality. As Durkheim says: "The ideal society is not far removed from real society; it is part of it" (*Elementary Forms of the Religious Life*). And also: "Only the human being is able to conceive the ideal and to add to what is real." Of course, we do not actually wish to make some addition to reality but to adjust things within the confines of the given, so that reality may be greater than what is given.

The way things are, being given and constructed, always seems contradictory. The ideal and utopian dimensions project a future factuality that contradicts that contradictory state of things. The present actuality says that we behave as wolves to one another. The future—utopian—actuality tells us that we are not condemned to suffer this situation forever, but that we are to be brothers and sisters, and that this ideal is inscribed in the potentiality of the already given and constructed reality. The given and the ideal together comprise reality in its truth, which both is and is to be revealed.

Religion is the more traditional and systematic form of organization of the utopian dimension of what most concerns humankind. For religion the world is not definitively lost. It is possible to recover it and to bring it to maturity. To die is not only to close one's eyes; it also means closing one's eyes to see better. There will be brotherhood and sisterhood between humanity and nature; a lasting communion between men and women; and a fusional encounter between God and humankind.

Religion is grounded in a hope that is also, at one and the same time, love of that which does not exist and faith in that which has not yet been experienced, as the Letter to the Hebrews rightly says: "Now faith means putting our full confidence in the things we hope for, it means being certain of things we cannot see" (Heb 11:1).

Rubem Alves, a thinker who has most proficiently analyzed the enigma of religion in contemporary Brazilian thought, says: "The purpose of religion is not to reflect the world. It arises from protest against the world that can be described and reflected by science. Scientific description, rigorously maintained within the boundaries of established reality, sacralizes the established order of things. Religion has the voice of a consciousness and conscience that can no longer find peace in the world as it is, and whose utopian project is to transcend it" (*0 enigma da religião*).

Religious and mystical experience is characterized by globality. It is concerned with the whole of life and its history and not merely with one sector. It does not grow or diminish as the process of secularization advances or wanes. The experience of the divine is a globalizing phenomenon because it can discern the presence of God both in secular space and within the confines of the sacred. The divine shines in and forth from everything.

The divine also has an integrative tendency apparent in all dimensions. It is wrong to think that religious experience belongs to a separate realm. It is separate from reason because it has access to a form of truth that is inaccessible to reason. It is separate from the secular realm because it is manifested only in the sacred; it is separate from the body because it is concerned only with the spirit; it is separate from history because it is interested only in eternity. Religious experience makes everything sacramental, because it is penetrated by and suffused with the presence of the divine. As the Japanese Buddhists say, everything can be transformed into *kami*, into the sacred and divine.

The divine is also transparent in the world process. The divine is not something added to human experience from outside. It is manifested through all experience. Everything has a depth that constitutes its other aspect and that mystery which refers to Mystery.

The experience of the divine is a global act on the part of the individual. It is a totalizing experience. It is not necessary to unite God and the world, for they are always present to one another. It is necessary to uncover their ties, for these constitute the divine transparency of the world. As St. Paul told the Greeks of his day: "He is not far from any one of us. Indeed it is in him that we love and move and have our being" (Acts 17:28).

Religious experience and its cultural expression, which is religion, is not pathological but salvific. It is a basic anthropological patrimony and is not reducible to another more primordial experience. It always exists in humankind in the most varied forms. Today it is emerging under a new form, as it tries to manifest itself in the form of expression most appropriate to the presence of the divine breaking out in various contemporary cultures.

The Return of Religious Feeling and the New Cosmology

Every religious experience is expressed in terms of a cultural code. It is a part of culture. It is influenced by the surrounding culture, which it also influences. Durkheim showed that religion is not confined to the forms of expression we know as ritual, worship, and doctrine (*Elementary Forms of the Religious Life*). It also gives rise to a cosmology, that is, to a form of discourse about the world. This is not a matter of scientific discussion, for that is not the concern of religion, but one of producing a global image of the world to indicate its connection with the divine dimension. Every cosmology represents God in its own particular way, as well as offering a globalizing, integrative, and sacramental understanding of the world.

In our Western tradition we are familiar with three major cosmological models. The typical cosmology of antiquity saw the world as a hierarchical, sacred, and unchangeable whole. Its characteristic metaphor was the ladder of being, with God at the top as the Supreme Being and Creator of the entire universe. We may say also that this was a theocentric cosmology.

The modern cosmology that developed on the basis of Newtonian physics, the physics of Copernicus and Galileo, and Cartesian scientific method, is dualistic. The world is divided into the world of matter and the world of spirit. Natural science analyzes the world of matter but leaves the world of spirit to philosophy and theology. From the scientific viewpoint, humankind in its continuum of fulfillment and frustration is of no interest. The only aspect of humanity and the world that counts as far as it is concerned is what is measurable. The rest is subjective and uninteresting from the angle of modern science.

The characteristic metaphor of this kind of cosmology is the machine. God is represented as the great Architect who planned the laws of this machine. They continue to guide things without any need for any kind of reference to their origin. It is the part of humanity to elucidate and establish their function. This cosmology is anthropocentric.

From the twenties a new cosmology emerged with the theory of relativity of Einstein, the quantum physics of Bohr, the indeterminacy principle of Heisenberg, the findings in theoretical physics of Prigogine and Stengers, and the contributions of depth psychology (Freud and Jung), transpersonal psychology (Maslow, P. Weil), biogenetics, cybernetics, and deep ecology. There has been a rapid transition from the industrial age to the era of communication and the rule of complexity. There is now a transition from a materialist world (linked to the production of material goods) to a post-materialist and spiritual world (interested in the integration of the everyday with the mystical dimension of things). In the face of this reality, the new synthesis reverts to a more primordial function of analysis: the holistic and organic vision has to complement the fragmented understanding of science. It is important to articulate the two ways of living and understanding the world: that proper to men and that proper to women. The new cosmology includes significant feminine elements, though in the past, in its cultural aspect, it consisted exclusively of masculine components.

The spiritual orientation of relations with reality as a whole, especially when faced with the ecological crisis, is becoming an imperative. The new cosmology proposes a vision of a unified but not hierarchical world, one that is organic, holistic, feminine/masculine, and spiritual. Living beings (and this is especially convincing from the viewpoint of quantum physics and the later version of the theory of relativity) are not juxtaposed or disunited. Everything is profoundly interrelated. Everything that exists is a complex bundle of energy in perpetual interrelativity. Matter itself represents one of the possible manifestations of energy.

Rather than talking of body and soul, matter and spirit, we should—logically—prefer to speak of energy and of life. The human being is no longer to be conceived as something over and above reality, indeed as dominating it, but is to be seen as a part of reality, as a participant in a whole, who has to preserve and respect the complexity and variety of that whole.

Above all, the category of spirit is profoundly renewed and deeply enriched by an understanding of modern cosmology. The spirit or soul is not to be understood as a part of the human being alongside the body, but as the totality of the human being in the sense of a living spring of vital energy. The spirit is not set over against the body but is opposed to death. There is no discontinuity between matter and spirit, between body and soul, but one between life (spirit) and death (the denial of life). By derivation, spirituality means that way of being which promotes life, its enlargement, respect for it, and protection of it. It also means obedience to and listening to that form of logic which is bestowal and gratuitousness of, and communion with, all life and all other forms of otherness.

The group of scientists at Princeton and Pasadena who are trying to renew science, philosophy, and religion, and who call themselves—somewhat ambiguously—the neo-gnostics, maintain as a fundamental principle of their basic cosmology that the world is dominated by the Spirit and made by the Spirit (R. Ruyer, *A gnose de Princeton* [São Paulo, 1989]).

The favorite metaphor of this new cosmology is that of play. As a European scientist and theologian says: "Play communicates the idea of complexity, of non-linear logic, but also of the essential implication and commitment of the players and of their creativity. The human being is no longer a passive spectator of a world from which he or she feels excluded" (M. Luyckx, *Religions et Ethiques après Prométhée* [Brussels, 1991], p. 23). This is an integrative form of cosmology.

What image does a cosmology of this kind yield? The dominant image of God is also linked to previous cosmologies. Every cosmology attempts its own characterization of the Presence to whom it bears witness amid the vast process of cultural change in which it is involved. This is not an easy process, but one that presupposes considerable experience and consequently more than one attempt to name the Ineffable.

When we look at present-day religious phenomena, it is not too difficult to see a number of instances where we are referred to God as Spirit. The Spirit is life and the giver of life, and life as Christian faith conceives and professes that Spirit. The Spirit is present in all processes of change, of inauguration of the new, and of the rise of diversity. The Spirit is communication and freedom par excellence. The Spirit is not imprisoned in religious institutions. According to St. John's gospel, the "wind blows where it likes, you can hear the sound of it but you have no idea where it comes from and where it goes. Nor can you tell how a man is born by the wind of the Spirit" (Jn 3:8) and "yet the time is coming, yes, and has already come, when true worshipers will worship the Father in spirit and in reality. . . . God is Spirit, and those who worship him can only worship in spirit and in reality" (Jn 4:23), that is, in freedom.

The Spirit is the Holy Spirit. Today we live in the age of the Spirit; of ferment and inspiration in the struggle for the liberation of the oppressed; in the women's movement as it seeks to remove the yoke of secular patriarchalism and tries to define women's identity in reciprocity with men's; in the great utopia that inspires the present changes in all fields of human activity; in the area proper to the great religions, as they return to their original experience; and in the charismatic fervor of sō many groups that are trying out a new way of life.

It is in this perspective that we have to consider the new popularity of popular religions in the world, above all in Brazil. This is an ambiguous phenomenon with a number of aspects that have to be viewed critically. It is difficult to assess the rapid spread of these religions and the infectious enthusiasm they sometimes arouse as merely due to economic suasions or to the ignorance of the masses. There is a positive side to such occurrences. What sort of people join these religious movements?

In the industrialized countries, they are groups that are deeply affected by the lack of direction in modern culture and are dissatisfied by the religious messages of the historical institutions. In the Third World, they are for the most part people deeply deprived of the basics of life and those who manage to survive the great social hardship that has decimated the masses. They are religious people. They thirst after God and hunger for bread. The historical churches cannot satisfy these vital demands. They are institutionalized; they have dogmatized their doctrinal heritage and bureaucratized their administrations. With difficulty, in their particular environments, they provide the conditions for a vital encounter with the living God. In the midst of poverty and privation they attract believers who are looking for God. Impoverished people, who are of no account socially, who are wanted by no one, not even by the politicians whom they have elected, people who are anonymous, disorientated in a society that expels and marginalizes them, the excluded in the underworld of the *favelas,* discover in these popular celebrations some measure of dignity, as well as a purpose in continuing to live, hope, and struggle. In so doing they speak directly to God and feel that God accepts them. Theirs is the conscious pride of being sons and daughters of God. They live for a while in an atmosphere of brotherhood and sisterhood that is denied them in all social instances. In these circles religion is not opium but liberation as opposed to the complete dehumanization that they suffer otherwise.

The Religious Factor and Cultural Distinctions

The concrete expression of the religious and mystical phenomenon runs through and across cultural differences. It does not take such points into consideration, remaining on an abstract plane and not acknowledging the limits inherent in all cultural expressions of religion.

I shall devote a few lines to an examination of Christianity in the light of the research that the Dutch sociologist Geert Hofstede and his group have carried out in forty countries; they investigate cultural differences and their religious expressions.

They have formulated four questions: What is the degree of verticality of a society (its "power distance dimension")? What degree of unconscious anxiety is there in a society ("uncertainty avoidance")? What degree of individual autonomy is there ("individualism")? And, finally, what is the impact of sexual differences on social roles ("masculinity/femininity")? (Cf. *Culture's Consequences. International Differences in Work-related Values* [London, 1991]; the same points, rehandled by M. Luyckx, *Religions et Ethiques après Prométhée*, pp. 16-22).

In this sector, the Latin culture in which a significant part of Christianity has taken shape (Roman Catholicism) is characterized by generally vertical, hierarchical, and centralized political structures and work organization. Catholics exhibit considerable self-assurance; they also tend to dogmatism, intolerance, traditionalism, and a meager acceptance of otherness (ethnocentrism). Above all, they reveal a high degree of individualism and of independence in encounters with the community, remaining very dependent on authority. In short, they tend to a masculine form of affirmation, without however succumbing to a full equivalent of Latin-American machismo. The super-ego of the Latins is incarnate in a strong personality, in the father, leader, and boss. The Latin way of resolving questions is to call on the advantages of hierarchy. Centralized power and individualism are united in a strong bureaucracy. Here everything depends on authority, but at the same time, in spite of the centralized, impersonal character of bureaucratic authority, there is a notion that freedom and independence are actually being asserted.

Anglo-Saxon culture, which has been affected by another significant part of Christianity (the Protestant Reformation) has various characteristics. The forms of government are more participative and democratic; this makes a more horizontal form of society. Such a culture experiences a low level of anxiety and serious social distress. It is more open to change and to the future. Individualism is very prominent but different from the Latin form, since authority is less distant, and there is a marked tolerance of otherness. Gender roles are more balanced, with a greater tendency to value the woman's role.

It is possible to analyze other world cultures, such as the Chinese, Japanese and Indian, as Hofstede has done. It is also very revealing to apply his principles in detail to African culture, as it is strongly evident in Afro-Brazilian religions. But that is outside the scope of the present inquiry.

In the foregoing I have tried to draw attention to the cultural dimension of religions. Many elements that are attributed to revelation, and so on, are made to seem unchangeable, as in vast sectors of Roman Catholicism, when they are actually no more than instances of a purely Latin cultural phenomenon. Papal infallibility, for example, is more an expression of a more emphatic form of self-affirmation, a mark of Latin culture, than a characteristic of Christian faith, which persisted for centuries without feeling any need to proclaim this dogma.

The Religious Factor and Social Justice

Religions have their common denominator in two basic points: the valuation of life in the form of compassion for it when it is devalued, injured, and oppressed. The return of the religious dimension today just has to face up to the misery that oppresses two-thirds of the human race. Religious unction must be capable of becoming sacred anger and a new kind of piety committed to social justice.

With the collapse of East-West confrontation, which was largely ideological (liberalism-socialism), the prevailing opposition today is that between North and South, which is economic and political in character. The contrast is one between the rich North where only 17 percent of humanity live, and the poor South, where 83 percent of humankind suffer.

Who listens to their cries? With the withdrawal of the socialist countries from international aid, there is little prestige to be gained for the richest participants in helping, and little equity and justice in the society of poor nations. The pressure is on religions and churches to act as more apposite locations for protests against the injustice of international relations and contrasts, and against the wasted products resulting from the rich countries' homogenized space and from the greed of international capitalism in its monolithic aspects.

If the churches and religions cynically keep their distance from this drama, and remain for the most part preoccupied with their own internal order, they run the risk of traducing the nature of their religious experience, which is always oriented to solidarity and justice, and of losing credibility as well as the respect they have always enjoyed in history.

This is the nub of the question: Up to what point are the Christian churches able to support the liberation movements of the poor, which possess in the shape of the poor themselves the subjects of their liberation? The leading circles of the Roman Catholic Church, as a result of their Latin inculturation, their strong centralism, and their pyramidal power structure, find it difficult to overcome their paternalist viewpoint. Even now the Vatican's position on this point remains unclear. Should they support the poor, provided that they do not take the way of revolution, only if the hierarchy itself guides the course of a liberation that is only religious and spiritual in the dualist sense of Greco-Roman tradition? Or should they safeguard the traditional paternalism practiced throughout history by the hierarchy which, in fact, has never resolved the problem of the poor?

The new religious movements run the risk of neglecting the question of social justice. The attempt to live the religious and mystical dimension is so absorbing that they become preoccupied with it, so that it represents their entire gamut of interests. Consequently, they are unable to assimilate or perceive other aspects of reality. The mystical dimension can degenerate into mystification, and the religious dimension can become escape to a private world or group life without enough interest in the socially responsible construction of justice or an appropriate ecological relationship.

The dehumanization of the quality of life on a world scale is a challenge for all religions. They will try to demonstrate their authenticity by assuming a committed and libertarian position in the face of this anti-reality. Ages characterized by religiousness are always appropriate to revolutionary trends. The mystic is not detached from history but committed to it as transformation, starting from a nucleus of transcendent meaning and a minimal utopian dimension which, inasmuch as it is religious, enables the mystic to be more perceptive than anyone else.

We cannot afford a self-satisfied religious or mystical movement. Of its very nature, it has to unite everything: the world with God, the conscious with the unconscious, immersion in its own inwardness with attention to the course of the world, and purity of mind with a just order of social relations. Only thus will there be a greater awareness of the global significance of events; only thus will there be greater indignation at abuses of power; only thus will there be a more insatiable thirst for life and freedom; and only thus will there be a much firmer bond between hunger for God and hunger for bread, so strong that it can ensure an encounter with what seemed ineffable— authentic testimony of the presence of the Supreme Being who visits us and comes to stay among us.

Religious Feeling and the Challenge of Science and Technology

Most contemporary religious movements are either premodern (and therefore do not pose the problem of science and technology), or have already made the break with modernity (and include the problem of science and technology in their process of reflection). Although these movements do not stress the crisis of instrumental reason, in an industrialized society they are in an environment that already takes the victory of scientific messianism for granted, as well as a general project controlled by reason. In this sense they are new and alternative, and no longer modern.

The historical churches are torn between loyalty to their own traditions, formulated in premodern terms, and the search for the right response to modern and new problems in this time of immense cultural change.

At Vatican II (1962-65), the Roman Catholic Church, for example, achieved a form of reconciliation with the critical and scientific thought of the modern era. It recognized the legitimate autonomy of science. But there has been an unswerving assertion by the hierarchy, especially under the last pope, of the absolute priority of humankind over the logic of science and technology, one that shows the hierarchy increasingly views knowledge and power as forms of domination of some nations over others as well as control of politics and of the world's wealth. Science and technology are seen as a form of human capital accumulated over generations, and therefore as essentially social in character. Consequently, they should not be monopolized by the industrialized nations to ensure their own levels of choice and hegemony, which require the adhesion and submission of other nations and peoples. We have to develop an ethical project concerned with international solidarity, and to promote and protect life so as to restrict the harm done by science and technology and to guarantee the survival of the creation.

In all this, Catholic thought remains largely based on a particular notion of natural law. Natural law, according to the Scholastic philosophers, accords with hierarchy and the reflection of the eternal law in every creature and in the human heart. Every individual is capable of discovering truth by the use of his or her intellect, and of encompassing it by the exercise of his or her will. Upholders of natural law are convinced that human beings, by virtue of the sheer intrinsic thrust of their being, are capable of inquiring into the nature of being, its truth, and its inward law, as well as the Supreme Being, and therefore are by nature ethical beings. Sin, however, has obscured the supernatural order and has injured the natural order. According to this way of thinking, however, human beings cannot decipher the natural law by the use solely of their unaided resources, and would remain in darkness were they to try to do so. God in his mercy, however, is the author of supernatural revelation as expounded in Holy Scripture; God has also established the magisterium, or teaching office, of the church as the authentic interpreter of the natural and of the supernatural revelation. Only that magisterium, without any risk of serious error, can read and interpret the natural law. Consequently the church is the absolute proprietor of ethical truth for all human beings, not only for baptized Christians.

On the basis of this claim, which was believed to be founded on revelation, the hierarchy of the Roman Catholic Church arrogates to itself the right to interfere in ethical decisions of society and to try to ensure that its decisions are accepted by everyone. It considers this view of things to be founded on natural law, which is present in all people, and that it must be comprehensible to, and therefore respected by, all human beings.

The hierarchy of the church seeks to provide a universal service of accurate interpretation of the interests and concerns of all people that will guarantee their common well-being and general happiness. The magisterial church believes that it has the right to interfere profoundly in such questions as abortion, birth, means of human reproduction and birth control, bioethical experiments, in vitro conception, donor fertilization and surrogate parenthood, organ transplants, and the manipulation of human embryos. In the church's opinion, doing so is a matter of safeguarding God's intended order for the creation.

Not a few theologians question this notion of natural law and the church's claim to enjoy the monopoly of ethical truth. This claim does not seem to accord with the message of Jesus, who showed absolute respect for human freedom. Moreover, this ecclesiastical vision presupposes an image of an authoritarian God, distrustful in dealings with men and women, afraid of human autonomy and love. This image of God is millions of light years distant from the image of the maternal God and infinite goodness that Jesus offered us.

In short, this concept of natural law does not leave enough room for the human freedom intended by God, the freedom by which human beings extend God's creative act, administering and transcending nature. Humankind is continually moving from an existential situation ordained by human birth and environmental culture (nature) to a situation that human beings create in exercising the freedom by which they define themselves and shape the world. Only by using this freedom do human beings become themselves.

Furthermore, we must always remember that nature is continually in the process of becoming. It is never completed. It is open to the future of God and to enrichment by evolution. Biblically speaking, the truth of nature is not so much what it is at this particular stage, but what it is intended to be in God's plan, which is realized progressively in history by means of its inward power and by the interventions of human beings.

In this perspective, everything is good that allows the person to blossom and develop, both in his or her inner depths and by opening out toward the universal other. That is bad which obstructs communication with self and with others, and which hinders self-giving and love in an egotistically self-centered way that excludes others. The ethical ideal, therefore, does not consist in the given situation (nature), but in the ideal situation to be brought about by transforming things as they are, for that is the Creator's design. Only at the end of this narrative will the prophetic word be fulfilled: "And God saw that it [everything] was good" (Gen 1:25).

When we analyze the official position of the Catholic hierarchy, from the kind of angle stressed by, for instance, Hofstede, it is clear that the Roman Catholic hierarchy takes up a quite centralist position on the ethical question. It is scarcely inclined to accept anything new and is not infrequently both imperiously obdurate and unwilling to take into account historical processes that reveal the previously obscured potentiality of nature. The proposition that the natural law is immutable owes more to an archaic premodern cosmology than to a proficient consideration of God's plan ("Behold, I make everything new!") for creation. The claim to have the monopoly of ethical truth is to be attributed more to the ideology of absolute power built up by pope and hierarchy in the course of history (its various stages can be reconstructed quite meticulously) than to the divine will, which is always directed to participation and to the promotion of freedom. Other Christian denominations, including the Orthodox, which is the closest to the Roman Catholic, do not interpret the testimony of the Christian scriptures in this imperial perspective. This only serves to confirm the peculiar and ideological nature of the official Roman Catholic interpretation.

In principle, the churches of the Reformation locate themselves within the perspective of modernity, because they came into existence in the same age in which the modern project was formulated. They have always looked on the scientific-technological process as a positive reality directed to the acquisition of human autonomy in history and liberated by God within the framework of a logic of gratuitousness. Consequently, they are very open to what is new. The ethical basis does not depend on a supposed immutable natural law but on hope of a kingdom of justice, integrity of creation, and of peace proclaimed by Jesus and slowly becoming apparent in history. Everything that helps to advance that kingdom makes up the basis of ethical good.

Today, by and large, two main tendencies are apparent in the scientific-technological process. The churches and religions have adopted decisive attitudes to it, starting from their respective ideas of the existing totality.

A first group tends to take to their ultimate consequences the possibilities of applying reason to nature. Science and technology, in particular, nuclear research, avant-garde physics, cybernetics, and biotechnology are capable of such far-reaching interference with the genetic code and in the transformation of nature as to be within reach of solving serious human infrastructural problems. Consequently, we now have a technocratic messianism that claims it will be possible to give everyone more than abundant food, housing, medical care, and leisure. We shall be able to satisfy the basic human needs that have caused such suffering for humankind. If they are not satisfied, there will be rebellion, violence, and a painful process of liberation. The longed-for liberation will be supplied by the new messiahs of science and technology.

The churches and religions acknowledge the importance of science and technology for the satisfaction of human needs and the promotion of life. Nevertheless, they tend to distance themselves from the solution proposed by this kind of messianism, which guarantees survival (providing bread) but does not sufficiently promote life (sharing in the production of bread). Human beings are not only creatures with needs; humans are also beings endowed with freedom. They are able to decide for and against, to decide and to accept the other's position, even when it is contrary to their own interests.

Human beings not only hunger after bread, a desire that can be satisfied, but thirst for beauty, a longing that cannot be assuaged, as the Cuban poet Roberto Retamar says. The logic of life is fulfilled not only in its own reproduction, but in creativity, communication, and communion. Human beings feel human not only when they receive public benefactions or the kindness of others. They wish to participate and cooperate, as subjects, in a collective and personal history; that is, they wish to bring about, by means of science and technology, forms of human participation at all levels. This is the process that humanizes us.

The second tendency considers that it has already entered the holistic, ecological, and spiritual phase. It subjects to relentless criticism the instrumental reason that has now become a veritable "earthly demon," because it threatens to destroy nature. The *hybris* ("arrogance") of its logic has to be restricted so that it can be included in a greater whole, where it can recognize various form of access to awareness that are not only scientific but holistic and symbolic. By sharing in these various forms of knowledge and self-fulfillment, human beings become integrated in the whole. They are harmonized and effectively transformed until they become cultivators of the garden of creation as well as its high-priests.

Religions help culture to take up this second position, with, considering the urgency of the matter, dramatic and positive consequences for all humanity.

The Religious Element and the Ecological Challenge: The New Song of Nature

The foregoing reflections take us straight to the very heart of the ecological question. We can no longer live under the threat of a modernity that conceives of, and wishes to use, science as a means of dominating nature as well as other peoples and cultures. In Canberra in 1990, at the Eighth Assembly of the World Council of Churches, on the theme of ecology and increased marginalization in the Third World, the final declaration said that technology should work *with* nature and its mysteries and not seek to dominate it (Final Declaration of the Assembly, 1:12).

The church played its part in the formation of the mentality that led to the present global crisis of the biosphere. It has not been sufficiently critical, and it has not used its theological armory as a counterweight to support a relational mentality of respect and concern for the creation. As the Canberra Assembly also remarked, the more theology has insisted on God's transcendence and distance from the material world, the more the earth has come to be seen as a mere object of human exploitation and as a "non-spiritual" reality (Final Declaration, 1:13).

In fact, all religions and—in our hegemonized Christian space—all churches, have their own contributions to make to the construction of, and to the education of those responsible for, a new alliance of humankind with nature.

All creatures, from the least to the most complex, form an organic whole. In religious terms we all proceed from the Creator's one and the same act of love. That means that there is a universal brotherhood and sisterhood among all beings. All creatures bear within themselves traces of the divine hand that shaped them, even if évolution was the way in which it happened. This means that creatures are sacramental. They are symbols of a Presence that inhabits the universe. As we have seen, this Presence has been evident in the form of the Spirit in creation. The old type of mysticism knew that the Spirit dwelled in creation and renewed the face of the earth.

Such wisdom suggests an experience of fullness and completeness. Reality is not empty, and the deity does not reside in some realm far away from it. God is present to and in reality, profoundly immanent, and becomes transparent through the medium of all created beings. This transparency is tarnished and obscured by the aggression that one creature, the human being, practices on other creatures, and, tragically indeed, on his or her own kind. What should prevail instead is ecological justice—respect for the otherness of beings and things and their right to continue to exist—and constant social justice, respect and concern for people, as well as the abrogation of those forms of oppression that are exercised through social relations.

The new alliance that humankind ought to make with nature must come above all from the heart. It is there that we allow the roots of aggression to take hold, so that a form of behavior is built up that transgresses the original concord among all beings. The drive to possess and the wish to control can take hold of the human being so relentlessly that desire becomes insatiable. The great ecological lesson of Buddhism and of Christian asceticism consists in asking whether we should not collectively restrict our desires. This is something incumbent on the profound ecology of the human heart. When reconciled with ourselves (mental ecology), we can, without coercion, live with our own kind (social ecology), and also with all other creatures (environmental ecology), as, indeed, brothers and sisters. Then humanity will behave with the respect and concern needed to promote a new era and the possibility of greater happiness for all.

Modernity implied disenchantment of the world, the reduction to the condition of an object characteristic of human experimentation, and the interference of technocratic reason born of an anxiety to dominate and to accumulate material goods. Today, however, the promise of a new historical era is marked by a perception of the whole as differentiated, organic, masculine/feminine, and spiritual, and as possibly enabling us to sing the new song of the world.

We cannot sing the new song of the world yet, or whenever we like. It will be heard when we enlarge our horizons beyond those of modern thinking and, by exercising our symbolic and mystic awareness, take into account the fact that the world carries both a message and a mystery. This mystery is glimpsed by scientists who have reached the limits of their understanding of matter, energy, and life. It is seen by Eastern and Western mystics as an energy system that is always relational and interactive, progressive and integrative, referring us to the supreme Spirit who penetrates and enlivens everything and renders it transparent.

The Eternal Message of Religion: The Other Side

The sociologist Durkheim concluded his famous work on the elementary forms of religious life with this statement: "Religion therefore contains something eternal which is destined to outlast all those specific symbols in which religious thought has been successively wrapped." Religious life does indeed possess an eternal quality. It does not fade away but is always present. It persists even amid the phenomena of modernity, but only in the form, as it were, of a solar eclipse. During eclipses the sun does not die. It merely passes out of sight and continues to exist behind the darkness.

The absence of God was a different form of presence through which the same human creativity was able to affirm the same power and truth. The Christian myth of creation, unlike the Greek myth of Prometheus, has always maintained that the human being is made a creator in order to prolong the creative act of God, and, being given the responsibility of a son or a daughter, to shape the creation with creativity and in freedom. God is present in *homo sapiens et faber*, not in person, but in and behind free and creative human activity. Here we see how theology discerns the value of the disenchantment and secularization of the world. As I have said, the withdrawal of God makes it possible for the human being to come into his or her own as a historical subject.

Today we are observing a new form of expression of the religious dimension. There is no return to the premodern world and its agricultural culture. The new affirmation inaugurates a new era. After the age of modernity we have an era of integration of all aspects of the human and cosmic dimension within a living, variable, organic, spiritual, and mystical totality: creation and nature in a vast evolutionary process. God does not appear as the antagonist of humankind. Instead, we and God cooperate in a reciprocal accession to and acceptance of one another.

The religious and mystical dimension bears witness to the other aspect of creation and nature; to, in short, the presence of the divine. Mystery and secret roots comprise the other side of things. To go on affirming this, in a thousand different ways, in the cultural codes of all eras, is the eternal aspect of religion.

The humanizing and liberating aspect of the religious dimension is revealed in its articulation with experience as a whole, and with all reality.

Malraux once said that the twenty-first century would either be religious or it would not be at all. The phenomenon of the return of the religious and mystical life reinforces our conviction that the twenty-first century will indeed exist and, so we trust, will manifest the reality that religions dream of: a reality of justice, peace, love, acceptance of differences, forgiveness, conviviality between opposites, and respect and love between human beings and toward God.

CHAPTER 3

The Nature of an Ecologico-Social Democracy

As far back as the beginnings of Greek philosophy it was realized that it is not sufficient to talk about various ways of governing a society (monarchy: government by one person; aristocracy: government by an elite; democracy: government by the majority). We have to choose the best way of living together and of governing, and to make this decision we need to understand the nature of society.

Society is not a thing, but a network of relationships among persons, their functions, their belongings, and their institutions. These relationships inevitably pose questions of responsibility; that is, of otherness, of anything that concerns some people and others. Ethics enters at this point.

Ethics comes into play in the relationships that human beings have, and it does so in a number of ways. Human beings not only have responsibility but are concerned to make the world as good as possible. This means that the ethical imperative goes beyond any specific achievement. It has a clearly utopian content. Deeds are good or best to the extent that they approach or are distanced from the utopian. Therefore, from the ethical and political standpoint, we have to find the *best* possible form of government.

In this context democracy has come to be accepted as the best way of organizing society. The basic presupposition is that what concerns everyone should be thought about, discussed, and decided by everyone. Social well-being, to be sure, concerns everyone. Therefore, everyone should be able to share in its formulation and construction. Democracy, basically, means a common building-up of the common good.

Different Forms of Democracy in History

History has produced various embodiments of democracy, along with various systems of government: constitutional monarchy, parliamentary supremacy, presidential rule, and so on.

The first is direct democracy. Society itself is organized democratically when all citizens share directly in decision-making. In Athens this applied to only a third of the population, the free men. The other two-thirds were made up of one-third slaves and one-third artisans and foreigners; these two-thirds were therefore excluded from the democratic process. This form of democracy presupposes a relatively small population, so that all can individually experience various forms of participation. Today direct democracy can be found in small communities, such as basic ecclesial communities and certain popular movements. On the social and political level the only currently valid example—in Europe—would seem to be the Swiss Confederation. Beyond small groups, democracy is difficult to achieve. Nevertheless, this remains the utopian referent of basic democracy.

The second form is representative democracy. Democracy in this sense is a way of organizing the state as the decision-making center of society. By voting, the citizens elect persons to represent them at various levels of authority. This is an indirect form of democracy. The people take part in it only when they cast their votes or state their opinion in a referendum. The daily run of politics is carried on by their representatives. In a class-differentiated society this representative democracy proves very imperfect. The stronger classes, particularly the ruling classes, can avail themselves of economic, ideological, and political advantages in order to elect their representatives. In their turn, these representatives will basically, though not exclusively, defend their class interests.

The third form is participatory or social democracy. Society not only has elected representatives but is organized in such a way that other social groups take part in decision-making: trade unions, nation-wide bodies such as the legal profession, the churches, industrialists, humanitarian or welfare organizations, universities, and the like. In this way the means of power are socialized, and democracy takes on a more day-by-day and dynamic aspect. The effect is to increase the citizens' sense of responsibility as active agents of society and co-builders of their common history.

The fourth form is democracy as a universal value. This derives from the well-structured application of participatory democracy. Here democracy becomes a value to be experienced not only in the form of political authorities (as relationships of power), but in all human groupings: in the family, seen in more egalitarian husband-wife and parent-children relationships; in schools, with efforts to break down the division between teachers and pupils; and in the churches and other social groups such as neighborhood associations, women's groups, trade unions, and political parties. For such a democracy to come about, we need a form of pedagogy that operates from the bottom upward and a willingness to listen to all those who wish to express themselves. We have to develop a basic attitude of welcoming differences, of listening to what others have to say, of accepting new elements as they appear, of being always willing to collaborate with and let ourselves be corrected and informed by others. The ongoing exercise of these attitudes creates a democratic culture.

Democracy as a universal value sends us back to the individual worth of every human person as the subject of inalienable rights. All citizens should be able to count on respect for their individuality as persons with their own gender, culture, ideology, or religion. Solidarity prevents national and historical differences from being treated as inequalities. This approach produces a society tending to become more egalitarian in the areas of recognition of rights and freedoms and therefore potentially less inclined to social conflict.

The Minimal Requirements
for an Ecologico-social Democracy

Today, a new form of democratic living is developing alongside these other forms, either as a universal value or as a more integrative way of organizing society. This new form is ecologico-social democracy.

We now have a higher level of global awareness, because we are collectively taking greater account of the ecological question. Ecology deals with relationships among persons and with their relationships with their environment. We are all concerned with the quality of life. We all feel the threat of destruction by nuclear disaster hanging over the planet. We are saddened by the fact of our systematic assault on nature, leading to the disappearance of animal and vegetable species. We are humbled by the sprawls of poverty encircling our great cities.

All these facts have to do with the question of ecology and are not divorced from our vision of democracy. We therefore need to ask for a democracy that is not only participatory and social, but ecological.

Environmental, conservationist, and ecological movements have ceased to be pressure groups set apart from others, and the only ones to raise the ecological flag. Today they are linked with movements of social concern, and the ecological dimension is becoming common to all of them. Just as, from the 1960s onward, the social and human sciences formed the necessary means of understanding and empowering political activities, so today ecology has to be taken into account in any theoretical understanding and social activity, if these are to make their expected contribution to assuring the integrity of creation, and in particular to safeguarding all forms of life, beginning with those that are most threatened.

First and foremost, ecology requires that we humans should advance beyond our anthropocentric viewpoint, which is deeply embedded in Western culture and continually reaffirmed by a certain type of interpretation of the Hebrew and Christian religious traditions, which see human beings as lords of creation and the universe. We believe ourselves to be the focal point of everything. We see all other beings as existing for our purposes, and all creatures as finding their meaning and praising God through human beings, at the mercy of human beings, to be used, dominated, and where convenient, exploited.

The understanding of reality behind the scientific and technological notion of modernity confirms this same will to dominate. Descartes, Galileo, Newton, and Bacon taught that knowledge is power and that power is dominion; that it means developing the capacity to subject all creatures with their brute strength to slavery in our service, as Descartes put it.

This conception has consecrated and underpinned the violence and aggression unleashed against nature since the beginning of the modern era (as witness the invasion in 1492 of what is now Latin America). It was present in the mode of development worked out then and still surviving today. This forms the greatest and strongest myth of humanity's collective conscious and unconscious: unlimited economic development without counting the ecological costs, such as destruction of ecosystems, exhaustion of the biosphere, plunder of nonrenewable resources (fossil fuels), and the like.

This model of aggression against nature has been reproduced in aggression against weaker peoples and militarily inferior civilizations. Afro-Latin Americans, for example, have been colonized and enslaved, their cultures overturned, and in many cases, destroyed. Besides Latin America, Africa and Asia have been victims of the aggression by European countries in which the agenda of the modern age was worked out. The same will to overpower and subject is focused on other human beings and nature.

Faced with such facts, ecological reflection has helped us to understand that the human race is part of nature and the biosphere, not the center of the universe. It exists in profound communion with all other beings. It is distinguished not by biological superiority but by the character of human beings as moral entities. This means that we can make free decisions, can choose the means by which we destroy other beings, but also that we can act beyond our own interests, to the extent of taking up the other's cause from the other's point of view. Indeed we are capable of assuming the responsibility for preserving nature and promoting all forms of life, especially those that are oppressed.

The most recent researches in biology and etiology show that the laws that have governed the process of building ecosystems comprise not the struggle for the survival of the fittest (Darwin), but a huge synergetic process based on collaboration and solidarity among creatures (James Lovelock, D. Sagan). The human race cannot deny its cosmic roots and its correlation to the conglomeration of bacteria and viruses that live in it and have been in existence for four billion years. The human psyche dates back millions of years and is inhabited by ancestral archetypes with roots sunk in life experiences going back to the first forms of life on the planet, 450 million years ago.

We are not the focal point of creation. We are not, as it were, its landlord, adopting the attitude of Adam, who gave all things their names and thus possessed them. We are here to serve as shepherds and custodians of other beings, and we are responsible for their integrity. We can use them, therefore, solely for our needs which, as those of human beings, always contain a measure of superabundance and gratuitousness. This is the true meaning of the biblical texts that speak of human beings as made in the image and likeness of God. As sons and daughters of God, and not as despots, we prolong the creative activity of God, cultivating nature, improving it, and multiplying it (as in the case of genetic engineering) responsibly. In this way, not only God is creator, but so also, by divine plan, are we.

Men and women are an end and not a means. But they are not the final purpose. There is no fixed central point, since all beings can be a center. What does exist is an equilibrium between life and death and an interplay of relationships embracing all beings, since some have need of others to exist and to subsist. We all exist thanks to others, with others, and through others. Together we make up the biosphere as a great integrated and integrating whole.

Next, we have to accept the otherness of all that exists in creation. Every form of being, animate or inanimate, has a value as such. It has its possibilities and limitations within the ecosystem itself. For human intelligence and affectivity, every being is a challenge to decipher the message of life, beauty, and rationality that it possesses in itself. All beings, especially living beings, deserve to be accepted and even respected in their otherness. No one has the right to seize and destroy what the vast process of evolution has spent thousands of years in producing. Everything that exists and lives has the right to exist and live.

The fact that every being is formed differently from me also lays an ethical obligation on me. Only human beings can bless this otherness, live freely with it, or wickedly destroy it. This is what grounds our ethical responsibility. The environment has its rights, and there is such a thing as ecological justice. Everything has the right to continue to exist, within the ecological balance. This right produces a corresponding duty in human beings to preserve and defend the existence of every being in creation. Today we call this the dignity of the earth (*dignitas terrae*), seen as a whole.

We also have to stress the reciprocity and complementarity existing between all human beings. Ecological balance sup-

poses that beings are reciprocal among themselves and complement one another in the whole. No being—above all no human
being—is sufficient unto itself. We have need of one another.
The proto-primary act of human culture, according to respected
biologists and anthropologists, would not have been using tools
to assure individual subsistence, but rather sharing food prepared by proto-hominids in a gesture of forming a community.
We are diverse in being able to exchange our goods and enter
into communion with others. We are diverse in order to be able
to be united.

Finally, in the light of these reflections, it is an urgent re-
quirement that we should understand the demands of a social
ecology. Social ecology studies human historico-social systems
in interaction with environmental systems. Human history is
inseparable from that of our environment, and from the type of
relationships that we have interwoven with it, in a dynamic
interplay of mutual involvement.

Social ecology relates social injustice to ecological injustice. The most numerous members of the human race are the
poor. Their relationship with the necessities for survival is distorted by the exploitation of their labor force. Poverty is seen
in the lack of an infrastructure for subsistence and a dignified
life: in a polluted water supply, poisoned air, unhealthy living
quarters, polluting transportation systems, and violent social
relationships. Since the human race is part of the environment,
social injustice goes hand-in-hand with ecological injustice.
We need to refine the concept of ecological justice, but without a minimum of social justice it is impossible to make ecological justice fully effective. The one involves the other. This
can be seen in the imposition by social ecology of the require-
ment of generational solidarity. Future generations have the
right to inherit a conserved earth and a healthy biosphere. Those
who come after us, human beings and others, have the right to
a future.

We are not allowed to destroy what we have not created. In
the future we must espouse not only a type of development

that reduces ecological damage to a minimum, but one that will be consonant with the resources of the natural environment (as Chico Mendes said of mining).

Finally, in the sphere of the rights of the environment, we should widen the meaning of the option for the poor to include an option for the most threatened of other beings and species. Here we should begin with the poorest human beings, those whose way of life is threatened with extinction, such as the Kaiapo, the Yanomani, and other tribes. We must also attend to animals such as the golden micalion, the iruapuro, the panda, and thousands of other disappearing species. In Amazonia alone it has been calculated that some fifty thousand species of insects and other creatures will disappear by the year 2000, thanks to the trail of devastation left by engineering and other projects that assault their habitat.

Faced with this prospect, what does an ecologico-social democracy mean? It is a democracy that accepts not only human beings as its components but every part of nature, especially living species.

A city is not made up only of inhabitants, buildings, roads, and public services. In the city, and far more in the countryside, there are trees, water, stones, hills, domestic animals, birds, earth, air, and the stars in the firmament, which we have a right to contemplate through an unpolluted atmosphere. How poor human existence would be without these elements, which are so rich in symbolic meaning since they populate our imagination and live in our very depths in the guise of inspirational values and archetypes. Carl Jung wrote: "We all need food for our psyche. It is impossible to find this sustenance in urban dwellings without a patch of green or a tree in flower; we need a relationship with nature; we need to immerse ourselves in our surroundings. My self is not confined to my body. It extends to everything that I have done and to everything that surrounds me. Without these I shall no longer be myself. Without them I shall not be a human being. Everything that surrounds me is a part of me."

All these beings, therefore, are also citizens, subject to rights, and should be respected as others, in their own otherness, in their own existence, in their own life, and in their communion with us and with our fate and their future, which may also depend on us.

For this new mentality to predominate, we urgently need to develop an attitude of respect, of veneration, of compassion, of brotherhood and sisterhood, and of tenderness and fellowship with the whole of creation in its infinite grandeur, infinite smallness, and infinite variety.

This is the political demand of an ecological education, if human beings are to learn to live with all other beings, animate and inanimate, as citizens of the same society. This is cosmic ecologico-social democracy.

Once this view prevails, we shall have broadened our own horizons, enlarged our hearts with sensitivity, and increased our knowledge, not as domination, but as a form of communion and participation in the existence of the other. We shall also have molded our wills as a force for collaboration with life and for service to everything that is tiny and threatened with extinction. Having largely overcome the promptings of fear, we shall feel that we are co-citizens of the same planet, and brothers and sisters in the same cosmic adventure, surveyed by the fatherly and motherly eyes of God.

PART 2

FROM ECOLOGY
TO GLOBAL CONSCIOUSNESS

The major problems facing us today are pollution, nuclear and bacteriological threats, deforestation and desertification, famine, and the demographic explosion. They all point to the central importance of the ecological question. This, in turn, is leading to the development of a new culture based primarily on a revision of our technological, political, and social outlook.

The new outlook of each of these aspects should link ecology to global consciousness. Only by doing this shall we be able to avoid the apocalypse and think in terms of a "new heaven and a new earth."

A true ecotechnology will have to divest itself of the model of unrestricted growth and make room for measures that aim to conserve the environment and reduce damage to it. Above all it will have to develop a new and alternative model of society.

In the present system, those who hold power ordain policies in defense of their own interests.

The new ecopolitics seeks to project a participatory, egalitarian, sharing society, one capable of combining imagination and analytical reasoning, technology, and utopia.

In our present society, the relationship between humankind and nature is one of continual warfare. Its logic means using force to obtain a degree of social order sufficient to guarantee the production of goods and privileges for a section of society, while the rest (the majority) benefit from them only to a secondary degree. The new model has to rebuild the social fabric.

Work has to be balanced with leisure time, efficiency with gratuitousness, and productivity with playfulness. We need to place a higher value on imagination, utopia, dreams, symbols, poetry, and religion.

In the Third World, the Christian base communities, inspired by liberation theology, have accepted this challenge, which acts as a driving force and as an ideal reference point independent of East-West and North-South conflicts.

CHAPTER 4

Globalization and Poverty

The collapse of socialism, with the fall of the Berlin Wall, the introduction of *perestroika* and *glasnost* in the former Soviet Union, and the general crisis in left-wing thought, has also made the churches ask a series of new questions about their actions and reflections. I shall now offer some reflections that start from the characteristic standpoint of the theologies of liberation. They give a high profile to the victims and vast oppressed majorities of the human race. Obviously I cannot deal with the whole question here. I shall ask only how globalization could become a reality in spite of the growing poverty in the world.

Where Does the Collapse of Socialism Leave Liberation Theology?

Many people believe—and this view is known to be shared by high dignitaries of the Roman Catholic Church—that, with the collapse of socialism, the theology of liberation will also disappear. In effect, they say, this theology was based on Marxism in theory and took the socialist model as its practice. What can we say to this?

We must always accept facts and learn from what they teach us. Socialism has indeed collapsed. I am not saddened by this.

On the contrary, I believe that its theory and practice already bore the seeds of its dissolution. In Eastern Europe socialism proceeded from the outside in, from top to bottom. It was built without the participation of the people. They lived with the consequences but did not share in the process. Socialism was authoritarian and patriarchal. It allowed neither freedom or democracy, whereas we know that its founders thought of *socialism* as the authentic term for real democracy, that of the majority.

Have capitalism, neo-liberal ideology, and the free market triumphed? Someone euphorically declared: *"Veni, vidi, Deus vicit!"* (I came, I saw, God conquered). This was obviously a hasty judgment. An equally authoritative voice could have replied: "Would it not be more realistic to acknowledge that *"Veni, vidi, mammona vicit"* (I came, I saw, Mammon conquered)? Probably.

In my opinion—and I am far from alone in this—the fall of socialism represents a victory for capitalism and the market economy only in appearance. In reality, it is much more of a triumph for the longing for freedom of the peoples in the socialist camp and a result of the contradictions caused by socialist regimes marked by the Leninist experience and the perversity of Stalinism, particularly in the economic and political spheres. Lenin's single-party strategy was totalitarian. It was imposed as a model for the whole of society and as the organizing power of the state. As such it violated the citizens' ontological will, in the form of their desire to participate in their own history and to be free agents shaping their personal and collective destiny.

But let us be fair. Socialism also banished famine. People from the First World cannot understand the meaning of this statement. Seen from the platform of the development of the First World, the socialist countries were backward and their societies overbearingly bureaucratic. But seen from the perspective of the Third World, socialism initiated a revolution that capitalism, as a whole, has still not achieved today, and from which humanity as a whole has profited. I repeat: socialism banished famine. No socialist country—Cuba, Russia, Syria—presents the scandalous phenomenon of slums, of thousands of children begging in the streets, of old people abandoned alongside the wealth and luxury of the few. In socialism the social fabric comes first. That is why there is better health care in Cuba than in any capitalist country, and a lower infant mortality rate in Havana than in Washington.

Socialist societies are more egalitarian. Let us take an impressive example. China has one million square kilometers more than Brazil, with a population nearly eight times as numerous (1.15 billion against 150 million). It produces virtually the same GNP ($340 billion). And yet China has a far more egalitarian social structure than Brazil. It is hard to find slums in China, whereas in Brazil eighteen million people live in *favelas,* or shanty towns. Children in China are fed and go to school. In Brazil there are twenty-three million abandoned children, of whom eight million live on the streets. Sixty million people in Brazil have only one meal a day; in China they eat three times a day. In Brazil there are forty million full illiterates, while half the people are functionally illiterate, barely able to write their names and spell simple words.

There is no denying it. Seen from the Third World, socialism has created more egalitarian relationships, with a sense of internationalism and solidarity not found in the capitalist sphere. It was not nourished by the exploitation of the poor, as capitalism is. It did not dominate the international market, which, seen from the impoverished countries, is a pirate ship.

But socialism did not succeed in banishing all forms of famine. In the words of Roberto Retamar, Cuban writer and poet: "Human beings experience two forms of hunger: the hunger for bread, which can be satisfied, and the hunger for beauty, which can never be satisfied." Socialism has not brought freedom. It has not satisfied the hunger for beauty. And who can say that freedom is incompatible with productivity, with efficiency, and with artistic creativity? Socialism controlled, repressed, and even murdered thousands of individuals who craved freedom. This is the ultimate reason for its fall. But we should not identify socialism with Stalinism, any more than we should equate the church of Christ with the Inquisition or the ex-Holy Office's current attacks on freedom.

Has capitalism triumphed with its market? Absolutely not! It is a system that has failed to deliver a single authentic benefit. There is no security for the poor, not even in the United States, where the number of those living below the poverty line is increasing. I see capitalism not as a utopia but as a scourge. It is an illusion to think that its benefits are for everyone. They certainly exist, but for capitalists. Outside their circle, crumbs fall to the poor, who will never be their equals.

To understand the significance of the capitalist accumulation of wealth, we need to examine its effects in the Third World. In Asia, Africa, and Latin America, large capitalist areas experience dependent and associate capitalism. There, the greater part of the population live in poverty and in conditions far worse than in the times of slavery, as far as nutrition, infant mortality, and life expectancy are concerned. Formerly, the poor felt oppressed but had hope. Now, they are still oppressed and, with oppression continually growing, many have also lost hope.

The system works only in countries already capitalist and industrialized. But their rapid development ravages nature and can never be made universal without producing a collective holocaust.

And what about liberation theology? Let me state clearly that liberation theology, from its beginnings, has never placed socialism at the heart of its practice and theorizing; it has focused on the poor as a collectivity living in a situation of conflict. Liberation theology has been concerned with socialism only as a form of mediation to advance the cause of the poor, as a historical alternative to the capitalism under which our people have suffered so much. And socialism has never been put forward as a model to be followed. Every nation has to build its own road toward socialism. I know of no liberation theologian who has been a member of a Communist Party. Socialism was seen purely as an historical reference point that could not be ignored. The real roots of liberation theology lie elsewhere.

Liberation theology was born of a twofold experience: political and theological. From the political point of view, it saw that the poor were a social and epistemological locus; that is, that their cause, their specific interests, their resistance and liberation struggle, and their dreams, allowed a particular and specific reading of history and society. At first this reading was denunciatory. It denounced the fact that present-day history is being written by a white hand and recounts the glories of the conquerors. This history represses the groaning memory of the conquered; it takes no account of the victims, and thus it is cruel and pitiless.

Liberation theology is also visionary. It dreams of possible transformations and human relationships in which human beings are friends with their peers and not with their executioners. Social praxis could make the dream a historical reality.

We can say with certainty that all the major questions that at present concern and inspire religions, plans for change and revolutionary processes, are linked to the dreams of the oppressed and the justice needed to put them into effect.

Liberation theology accepted this as fact because Christian militants occupied the same trenches as the poor, in trade unions, popular movements and—sometimes—guerrilla warfare. In this context they asked themselves, How can we proclaim that God is Life and Father in a world of destitution? Only by transforming this anti-reality into a worthy reality can we redeem the truth of faith that God is Father and Mother of all and defender of the poor. Starting from this point we can understand the need for Christians, including theologians, to become involved and to take a militant part in the processes of change.

The second, theological, experience occurred in order to deepen the first. The base Christian communities learned that the best way to interpret the pages of scripture was to compare them with the pages of life. This comparison revealed a truth that runs through the Christian scriptures from start to finish: the close connection among God, the poor, and liberation. There God is testified to as the living God, giver of all life. God is not like idols that are dead and demand sacrifices. This God, by nature, by essential vitality, is drawn to those who weep; God seeks to remove the oppression from their lives. This God makes the resistance and liberation struggles of the oppressed God's own. The biblical God is one who hears the cry of the Hebrews in their servitude in Egypt and sets them free. This God hears the cry of Jesus on the cross and raises him up. Today this God legitimizes the liberation struggles of millions of human beings who no longer accept their oppression but claim life and liberty. God takes their side, not because they are good, but because they are oppressed. They can put their trust in God. God's plans work through the desires of the poor.

This intuition has given rise to a spirituality, a practice of entry into popular struggles, and to a theology. In effect, liberation theology draws water from the well. On the basis of this struggle on behalf of the oppressed, liberation theology adopted certain arguments from the Marxist tradition. These arguments helped—and still help—to overturn the perverse logic of gain paid for by misery and the dehumanization of the masses. Beginning with suffering under the capitalist order (which is not order but disorder), Christians inspired by liberation theology put forward the idea of democratic socialism as a possible historical alternative, in order to acquire strategies and practices of working that were not only more worthy of human beings but generated more life for all.

Latin America is the only continent in which theologians are subject to police surveillance, arrested, tortured, and murdered—as happened a few years ago to our Jesuit brothers in El Salvador. But what is there in this theology that instills such fear into the capitalist system and induces its supporters to share the mortal fate of so many sons and daughters of their people?

Latin America is a continent signed with Christendom, which was imposed along with colonization. Simply because it is a continent full of Christian references, theologians are murdered in it. It is not Marxism that makes the system afraid. Society and some ruling elements in the church are afraid of God. They are afraid of this God who liberates, who upholds the struggles of the oppressed and gives them courage to accept the final sacrifice. They cannot accept the fact that the option of the poor against their poverty springs from the heart of the Christian faith and from the very essence of the biblical concept of God. They would prefer it to originate in Marxism and the ideologies of the Left. This is the incomprehension and the calumny that the doctrinal authorities in Rome are spreading throughout the world. They fear the Christian affirmation that, because of God's tender love for the poor, because of the gospel, and because of the faith of the poor, I have every reason to postulate a change of society, in which the poor themselves will become the protagonists. Because I myself have affirmed the need for this in the internal workings of the Roman Catholic Church, I have had to submit to a doctrinal trial in Rome and to successive punishments.

This liberating vision, which springs from the trappings of faith itself, also breaks the monopolistic hold that Marxism had on revolutionary utopias. With this vision, a Christian could be a revolutionary. Furthermore, this libertarian idea frees Christianity from the conservative slavery to which the capitalist order had subjected it, reducing it to the permanent enemy of Marxism and the processes of change. The theological debate about liberation theology is irrelevant. It serves to hide the actual debate, which is political. What we really need to know is which side Christianity is supporting in the balance of historical forces, now: the side of those who want to maintain the existing order because it favors them; or the side of those who seek to change it because it punishes the poor excessively. The great majority of churches in the Third World have understood the question: If we do not take the side of the wretched of the earth, we become enemies of our very humanity. By losing the poor, we also lose God and Jesus Christ, who chose the side of the poor. Then we are without any historical relevance.

As long as there are oppressed people in the world, there will always be discerning spirits who go out to fight for freedom. They will make Christianity not a totem legitimizing the aristocratic powers of this world, but a mysticism of liberation for the oppressed millions. Those who reflect on this practice will be doing liberation theology.

What future is there for socialism? From where I stand, from the viewpoint of the victims, that is, I answer: The factors that led to the rise of socialism two hundred years ago are still in existence. They are now worldwide—and growing. For the poor, for those who are held back in underdevelopment, or social democracy, for basic human rights such as the right of all to life and to survival, capitalism offers no security. In Latin America, capitalism, with or without elections, is not democratic. When the ruling classes see the capitalist order threatened, they soon call in the military. To save capitalism they will violate every existing personal, social, and political right.

We have to seek hope elsewhere. Then we turn to the socialist dream. The crisis of a particular type of socialism will not be enough to stifle such noble and humanitarian aspirations.

Socialist aspirations are rooted in the deepest strata of the political beings that we humans are. They feed dangerous visions. Stripped of hegemonic power and purified from the vices of its historical embodiment, democratic socialism will surely find its natural place in the peripheral and oppressed nations of the Third and Fourth Worlds.

I should like to add one thing: Human problems are spreading on a global scale. This means that the solutions too have to be worldwide. They will increasingly become the fruit of a vast process of socialization and democratization, which will also have a cosmic dimension. We have to learn how to live with stones, plants, animals, and the stars as new citizens of the human city.

Socialism, which by its nature puts the collective whole at the foundations of its thinking, can stand for the great alternative of a naturalized humanity, determined to survive in a sphere of togetherness. I refuse to believe that we humans are condemned to mutual exploitation, to living obsessed with gain at the expense of others, and sentenced to egotism.

In Search of an Alternative, Integral Modernity

There is no denying the fact that the disintegration of the so-called socialist camp, the period of *glasnost* and *perestroika*, and the end of the Cold War have produced a crisis in the agenda for changing society. We have only to look at the crisis among left-wing intellectuals and the confusion in movements that have their bases among the people. At the same time, the joy of the exponents of the capitalist order knows no bounds. They feel triumphant and say to one another, "History has proved us right." Everything is now ruled by market forces. They are the overall reality, the new divinity. Anything outside the market might as well not exist. Those not subject to the market might as well disappear. There is even mention of the "end of history." But of which history? The European myth is to speak of modernity and post-modernity. Not only do we have internationalization, but now globalization as the planet-wide extension of the means of production and information, and exchange technology. No one speaks of imperialism any more, for it has gone out of fashion.

What is actually happening? A new imperialism! I state this without apology. We are witnessing a new empire of the type of rationalism, of development and the meaning of existence conceived in the belly of the merchant classes at the beginning of the modern era, and now disseminated throughout the world.

What alternative is left beyond the idea of development other than to extend it to the farthest confines of Amazonia or Polynesia? The same logic that destroyed the "witness cultures" of Latin America in the sixteenth century has continued its devastating course to the present. Iberian colonization reduced the population of Mexico, in eighty years, between 1519 and 1595, from 25.2 million to 1.37 million. It was the greatest genocide in history, killing twenty-five inhabitants for every one left alive. Hear the testimony of the Mayan prophet Chilam Palam on the first years of evangelization: "They, the colonizers, came to teach us fear. They came to trample the flowers. So that only their flowers could live, they destroyed all our flowers."

Today, in the name of modernity, Latin American governments are bringing the logic of domination up to date through the grandiose schemes of multinational corporations from Japan, Germany, Italy, and the United States. The cost of this and of a foreign debt that cannot be repaid is more and yet more deaths. In Brazil alone a thousand children die of hunger every day. We have never seen death on such a scale as today, caused by unemployment, low wages, disease, and violence. Dozens of still surviving indigenous peoples are rapidly disappearing. In this way, we shall lose forever forms of humanity of which we have great need.

We should heed the voice of one of Brazil's greatest indigenists, Villas Boas: "If we claim that the purpose of our stay on this earth is to accumulate wealth, then we certainly have nothing to learn from our indigenous peoples. But if we are looking for integration between generations, for a peaceable alliance with nature, and a balance between production and consumption, we can certainly learn wisdom from them."

I am not against modernity as seen in its two embodiments in history: on the one hand, bourgeois modernity, which created industrial society, the market and consumption, as well as liberal-representative democracy; and, on the other hand, the proletarian modernity that introduced a new historical agent to the hegemony of society, the builders and agenda of socialism, now falling apart in its Marxist-Leninist version. These two forms of modernity were opposed to one another for decades. Now we have to construct a convergence between them. I am postulating an alternative and integral modernity that will conjoin the vast patrimony of science and technology (the fruit of bourgeois modernity) with social democracy, for the good of all humanity (the meaning of proletarian modernity) in an enhanced awareness of a common destiny.

For this to succeed, we need a new world revolution. Who now talks of revolution in the First World? The word has been relegated to the limbo of political theorists and party bosses. It is valueless, a coin out of circulation. And why should it have any value? The militants of the First World, many of them belonging to the repentant Left, ask: Why put our prosperity at risk, especially after so many wars? The idea of revolution has been consigned to the archaeological museum of politics. Yet, though it has lost its prestige, we must still talk of revolution as the way out of the wretchedness of the vast majorities.

The First World does not have the powder to ignite the idea of a new revolution, which today needs to be universal in scale. I must affirm, without any reticence, that hope does not reside here. Hope for the First World lies in reproducing its present prosperity and conserving ongoing development. Therefore it thinks of the existing order and not of possible alternatives, and the mind of the existing order, however progressive it may seem, is always politically conservative. Being conservative at present implies accepting the condemnation to exclusion and even to death of the major part of the human race, who are outside modernity and its benefits.

Can we make India, China, or Latin America into what Germany or Italy are today? The models of society and development that prevail nowadays cannot be universalized. Nevertheless, we have to survive as a human race. This means that profound worldwide changes are needed, embracing a new economic order, a new concept of ownership, and different social and ecological relationships—in short, a new humanity.

Center of Gravity: The Poor Two-thirds

Who are the bearers of a new hope? The collective poor who live in a state of conflict. The world's poor are condemned to be the soil of a new hope in history. There is no merit to them in this; it is their mission to usher it in in the name of all and to the benefit of all humanity. They alone, in effect, are in a condition of being able to dream. The present does not belong to them. Their past is the past of their masters, which they had to assimilate. All that is left to them is the future.

It may seem strange to speak of dreams and utopias. I believe, however, that we need to redeem the outstanding social importance of dreams and of the creative imagination. This, according to Pascal, is our domestic lunacy. But this lunacy is not the opposite of reason. On the contrary, it represents a greater reason, one undomesticated by the system and uncontrolled by authority. We might say that modern reason is caught in the nets of economic and political power. Through imagination, society and the oppressed dare to transcend their prison and envision a world different from this perverse one that denies them participation and life. This imagination belongs to those who hunger, to the sick, to those tied down by a thousand chains. This imagination has its own historical agent, the sum total of those who make up the universe of the two-thirds of humanity who are marginalized and socially deprived. These shout to the center from the periphery. They want to reduce distances. They want that minimum of fairness without which we cease to be human. Finally, they want an end to the division between North and South, between rich and poor, and to move toward a humanity that is finally reconciled to itself.

These are the dreams of the oppressed. They do not dream of becoming greater powers and dominating others. They do not dream of unbridled consumption and the associated lack of solidarity. Their dreams are tied to the basic structures of life and of the continuance of a truly human life. Therefore they relate to work, to health, to housing, to minimal leisure, and to the culture needed to communicate. Technically, these essential goods could be available to everyone. The fact that they are not is due solely to a lack of worldwide political will.

At present, with the East-West, capitalism-versus-socialism confrontation over, and the North-South, rich industrialized nations versus poor nations kept in underdevelopment, it is possible that the worldwide problem of the poor will become the center of political gravity. In effect, the poor will certainly become the world's point of balance, because they will be the major threat to any system that excludes them.

It would be intolerable for any ethic to help make the dualism in the world worse: an increasing accumulation of wealth and consumer spending on the one hand, and the wretchedness and destructuring of three-quarters of the human race leading to increasing slavery, on the other hand. If bridges of solidarity between the rich and poor worlds and their political systems are not built, the rich nations will be obliged to build endless Berlin walls to defend their society of plenty against invasion by the famished who will be beating at their doors. The crumbs from the rich man's table will hardly feed them and the dogs. Figures show that 13 percent of the world population lives in the rich countries and 87 percent in the wider South. If the poor are not helped with their basic needs, what guarantees of peace and comfort can there be for the rich?

Instead, therefore, of globalizing the market and profit mechanisms, we need to globalize other cultural values, such as solidarity, collective compassion for victims, respect for cultures, sharing of goods, effective integration with nature, and feelings of humanity and mercy for the humiliated and offended.

Does all this sound utopian? Of course it does. But utopia is part of reality. It is not a flight from reality, but the discovery that we are at the edge of history, that history always remains open, and that it is possible to live together in better ways. Human beings, men and women, are not sons and daughters of enslaving necessity, but of liberating joy. By yearning for the impossible we become open to achieving what is possible.

The ancient Romans cherished an ecumenical ideal that enabled them to confer the dignity of Roman citizenship on all inhabitants of the Empire, from Greeks to barbarians, with all the concomitant advantages. Today we should postulate recognition of human citizenship for all the inhabitants of the earth, since the great majority are treated as non-persons because they were late in arriving at the type of development invented by the West; they are treated as economic zeros in the marketplace.

For this recognition to succeed, we urgently need *glasnost* and *perestroika* in capitalism. What quality of life does capitalism actually produce? What type of democracy is it planning? One cut off from the people by political institutions, by the vote, and by bills of rights that do not extend into the economic sphere, protected from free choice and market forces? In effect, liberal democracy stops at the factory gate. Private property is detached from the sphere of the common good.

The globalization of human destiny shows the urgent need to deal with a question still more basic than that of socialism. This is the question of democracy—democracy known only, or not so much, as a system of government, but as a universal spirit and value. This path offers a possible future for humankind. Democracy, as envisaged now by so many groups in Latin America, is based on the co-existence and articulation of five founding forces: participation, solidarity, equality, difference, and communion.

Participation has to be guaranteed in the first place. Rather than seek an egalitarian society directly, today we are seeking a society that is participatory on every possible level. This participation is not reduced to a simple integration into the status quo, but means a share in establishing new relationships and in bringing about situations not yet tried.

In second place, solidarity at all levels becomes important, especially in the international perspective. It is the capacity to include others in one's own personal and social interests and to enter into the world of the other in order to uphold it, especially in relation to those most punished by life and history, the most needy.

In third place, as a result of participation and solidarity, a greater social equality comes into being. Societies of the past were characterized by inequality and exclusivity. To the extent that individuals share in and experience solidarity, more symmetrical and therefore humanizing relationships emerge.

In the fourth place, we try to accept, defend, and promote differences. These constitute the riches of every individual and of cultures. The samba is fine, no doubt, but alongside this we have the chanson, country music, rock, opera, Gregorian chant, and classical symphonies. Think what a disaster it would be if heavy metal were decreed to be the only acceptable form of music! The diversity of musical forms makes up the richness of music as a whole. In the same way, sharing in and valuing singularity ensure that differences do not degenerate into discrimination and inequality. The capitalist way of thinking and acting tends to stress differences to the point where they become inequalities. Socialism, on the other hand, tends to abolish differences, seen as inequalities, and to homogenize everything, killing creative capability.

The last element is communion. Communion is the capacity for establishing interpersonal relationships, for nourishing spirituality, in the wider sense of the term used by Gorbachev in his interviews, meaning an appreciation of ethical, aesthetic, and religious dimensions, which are all factors that build up human community. Communion is an anthropological rather than a religious capacity. It reveals a living transcendence in human beings, who are not defined by society, but constantly open upward and outward, building new meanings to life.

The construction of democracy can occur in families, in schools, unions, churches, the state, and society. It is an ever open and incomplete process. We seek a healthier humanity, one more worthy of life, so we want greater democracy. With greater democracy, built on these powerful forces, we can believe that the future will bear greater hope for the oppressed of the world and for all people.

The poor are crying out. This is their power and their right. But who today is listening to the cry of the oppressed coming from the heart of the earth? We need a worldwide mental revolution, a worldwide revolution in our habits, and a worldwide revolution in society for this cry to be heard effectively and to be listened to.

If the Christian churches and other religions today have any social relevance, this will lie in not allowing themselves to remain deaf to the clamor of the oppressed; in acting so that this clamor is heard in all spheres of the world; and in making this clamor find loudspeakers that will allow it to be heard effectively.

Liberation theology, among whose practitioners I count myself, is trying to make its contribution. Out of solidarity it puts itself in the place of the poor. It denounces the perversity of widespread poverty to the authorities. Thereby it associates itself with the poor against their poverty, not seeking riches that are themselves unjust, but looking simply for justice. The dream is one not of either a poor society or a rich one, but one of a just and sharing life for the whole of creation. This dream can become reality. If we dream it alone, it will be illusory, but if we dream it together, as a song from the base communities says, that is a sign of the solution.

Therefore, my friends, let us try to dream together, to dream quickly, and to dream in collaboration with one another.

CHAPTER 5

Society and Religion
after the Collapse of Socialism

We have to think in accordance with the facts and to learn continually from history. What challenges do the following events still pose to liberation theology and the base communities: the overthrow of the last traces of Stalinism through *glasnost* and *perestroika* in Russia; the massacre of young people demonstrating in favor of democracy in Tiananmen Square in Beijing; the collapse of central state control in Eastern Europe; and the defeat of the Sandinistas in Nicaragua which, together with Cuba, had kept the revolutionary flame alive in Latin America? These events give rise to three questions:

1. For groups dedicated to social change, the utopia of socialism has always been a dream accompanied by the expected overthrow of capitalism. With the crisis and collapse of "real socialism," what alternative to capitalism is there? Has this in fact finally triumphed?

2. What validity does the vocabulary of Marxist theory still have for understanding society, particularly categories like "productive forces," "development of capital," "social classes," and the like? Marx never thought of the *Lumpen* (ragamuffins) as an agent of social change. Today they decide the outcome of elections, generally voting for populist candidates who sup-

port the capitalist order—the very order that creates and excludes the *Lumpen*. How should we view this situation?

3. Christians contributed to the triumph and consolidation of the Sandinista revolution. Today the Sandinistas have been deprived of power through a democratic vote. A situation like this has a significance beyond Central America, which is always in a state of flux, and poses a basic question: What is the position of Christians in processes of structural change? And in revolutions and changes of social models?

Let us try to face up to these three questions without subterfuge.

Socialism Has Not Gone into Exile: It Is the Dream of Liberated Humankind

Marx never intended socialism to be a pure and simple alternative to capitalism, but the realization of ideals proclaimed by the bourgeois revolution: liberty and dignity for citizens, and their right to free development and to a share in building a collective and democratic habitat. Marx's concern was this: Why does bourgeois society not succeed in achieving the ideals that it proclaims for all? It produces the opposite of what it intends. Workers should be subjects of their work. Instead they have become its objects, because the effort of their work is turned into objects, becoming goods for the market, for which they receive a wage. The political economy should satisfy human needs (food, clothing, housing, communication, and so on). Instead, it follows the demands of the market, which are often artificially controlled. In capitalism, everything becomes a product, something with which to make money—from the most sacred elements such as religion and spirituality to our daily bread, or rice and beans. All human activity is what it produces and is valued in monetary terms. Objects become subjects and subjects objects. In other words, characteristics such as life, strength, and power are attributed to objects, whereas subjects are described in terms of objects. People's labor is expensive, good value, and so on.

For Marx, the non-realization of the ideals of the bourgeois revolution was not due to bad will on the part of individuals or social groups, but was the inevitable consequence of capitalist means of production. This pattern of production was based in the first place on private ownership of the means of production (capital assets such as land, factories, and machinery), with the results this produced in the organization of political systems, law, education, and social aspirations. In the second place, it was based on the subordination of labor to the interests of capital. This situation divided society into social classes, with opposed interests. The higher the wages of the workers, the lower the profits of the owners, and vice versa. This revealed the antagonism of class interests, which in its turn produced the class struggle.

In the capitalist order, individuals, willingly or not, tend inevitably to become dehumanized and structurally "superior" in relation to others, since all have to think of their own interests.

What solution did Marx envisage? Let us change the system of production. Instead of private property, let us introduce social property. But be careful, Marx warned. Changing the system of production is still not the solution to the problem. Socialization does not guarantee a new society. It merely creates the conditions in which it can come into being. Social property is only a means for changing human relationships, limited to affording the possibilities for individual development. Individuals will no longer be means and objects, but ends and subjects, brothers and sisters together complementing one another in the building of a truly human society.

Once these conditions have been established, citizens should want the new society and live effectively in new relationships. Otherwise, there will be no revolution. Consequently, we must not only consider how structures work, but above all attend to human subjects both as a collectivity and as individuals. Hence

Marx's famous dictum: "History does nothing. . . . It neither struggles nor fights. It is above all the human person, the actual, living human person who acts, possesses and struggles. It is not just 'history,' as though it were a person in itself, that uses human beings as means to achieve its aims. History is not something set apart from other activities of human beings in pursuit of their aims."

This, then, was socialism as Marx and Engels saw it: a last stage before the arrival of the great new utopia of communism, to which all citizens would contribute according to their means and receive according to their needs. But that is the great political dream of humanity, and this is not the place to analyze its possible realization in history.

For Marx, the victims of the capitalist system, the wage-earners, would be most affected by, and become the protagonists of, this transformation. They, therefore, would be the natural bearers, alongside other allies, of the standard of socialism. Why were they not victorious? Without wishing to discuss all possible obstacles put in their path, we can point to a very prominent one: Lenin's creation of the one-party state. The single party sees itself as the "guide and educator of the masses." It alone organizes the whole of society and the state, eliminating autonomous popular participation, which it replaces with a huge body of "cadres." It blocks social democracy, introduces a vast mechanism of social control, and generates a bureaucratic state, which is not participatory. In this respect it is pertinent to recall that Eric Honecker, the president of the former German Democratic Republic (East Germany), coined the expression "real socialism" (*der real existierender Sozialismus*, or socialism as it actually exists).

There is possibly nothing closer to the structure of real socialism than the structure of the Roman Catholic Church, apart from the variation in self-understanding. The Roman Catholic Church also features a great ideal, Jesus' dream of a community of brothers and sisters, in which creatures and possessions are held in common: the community of "one heart and soul" of

Acts 2 and 4. In reality, what exists today (*die real existierende Kirche*, or the church as it actually exists) is a pyramidal religious society made up of unequals (clergy and laity), which cannot simply be identified with the church of Christ. It is a version of Jesus' dream worked out within the ambit of Western, European culture. It is deeply marked and limited by political structures inherited from feudalism, with the positive aspects and the defects of that descent. The church also has its party (its social class), consisting of the clergy, who do not amount to 1 percent of its faithful.

Around the year 1000 this party carried out a coup-d'état. It assumed all power in the church-community. From then on it has organized everything, decided on everything, and created a discourse of self-identification with the church. The clergy (pope, bishops, and priests) have become purely and simply synonymous with the church.

In spite of due variations, the structures of these two totalitarian and authoritarian bodies, real Catholicism and real socialism, converge to a certain extent, even in details (for example, the ideological leader is equivalent to the prefect of the ex-Holy Office, with the same function of control and punishment) and both obey the same logic.

Obviously we are dealing with human constructs and, in the case of this aspect of the Catholic church, it would be erroneous to consider it divinely instituted, largely out of respect and veneration for the divinity of the church, which should not be manipulated to legitimize special group interests—in this case, those of the church's one party, the clergy.

To return to the main argument: How far was the society that defined itself as socialist actually socialist? Scarcely at all, by the criteria of the proponents of social ideals. They dreamed of a democratic socialism, starting with the masses of the people, that would include all the values of the bourgeois revolution, create new ones, and render them universal. But that did not happen.

We must not lose sight of those great ideals that have become crystallized in the idea of socialism. They are among the most ancient dreams of the human race. The crisis of a certain type of socialism (state run and authoritarian) should not be allowed to extinguish any hope of more human social conditions. Capitalism has not triumphed. What has proved victorious is the will to participate and live together democratically. No one will be so inimical to his or her very humanity as to accept that the final verdict of history is that we should live as wolves and not as mutual friends.

Today, though purified of their vices and shorn of their hegemonic power, socialist ideals have not gone into exile. They have found their place in their natural habitat; that is, in the poor and oppressed countries of the Third and Fourth Worlds.

We need to learn the lesson of history. The society we wish to build must be configured to the many-sided nature of human beings. They possess an individuality, a family, a community, and both a social and a transcendent dimension. The ownership of property should be adapted to these dimensions—not only private property, and not only social property, but various types and combinations that respond best to human requirements. Given the importance of the social dimension today, social ownership will certainly predominate, but it should coexist with other forms, with the conditions obtaining at different levels of society, and with political and cultural development, and so on.

It is, furthermore, a grace of the Spirit if Christian churches and other world religions make connections with socialist movements and discover a cohesion between religious propositions and socialist dreams. Either humankind enters on a vast process of socialization, with an open-ended and therefore cosmic democracy (living together with the stones, the plants, the waters, and the clouds, as brothers and sisters), and thereby preserves the sacred gift of being and life for all; or it runs the risk of a nuclear holocaust. And this time there will be no Noah's ark to save anyone, capitalist or socialist, atheist or believer.

What Is True Remains True

To make the new socialization more appropriate to human nature, and thus achieve the ideals of the bourgeois revolution that capitalism frustrated, Marx proffers an analysis of capitalist modes of production. What matters for capitalism is production and consumption in the form of private acquisition. The positions individuals occupy in the productive process determine their social class. Since there are various positions, there are different classes. Each class also represents a sum total of particular interests and defines for itself the subjective collectivity of those who belong to it. Since the interests of one class conflict with those of another, class struggles arise, as we have seen.

This makes capitalist societies intrinsically conflict-prone and rigid. Each class puts forward its own way of understanding, feeling, and self-inspiration; its own form of family, community, and social relationships. The head, in fact, thinks from where it has set its feet; and the heart feels from the type of relationship it has developed socially. Marx was not only an analyst of capitalism and an architect of socialism. He also introduced a philosophical outlook into socialism. He wanted it to know how human society was constructed. He produced an analysis that is among the most consistent in the history of thought. All serious students of society (including theologians) have to take account of Marx, and analytical thought has still not succeeded in assimilating him completely, since he conceives the basic dimensions of the social construct as a flexible (dialectical) process.

Marx, for example, realized that three basic powers come into play in any society. They are always interconnected, for each requires, presupposes, and includes the others in a dialectical process. These forces are economic power (responsible for the production and reproduction of material life); political power (the way in which power is distributed and the organization of social relationships, especially in connection with access to the goods necessary for human life); and symbolic power (the means of representing the world through symbols, ideas, religions, mystiques, and values). When we relate these three powers to one another, according to Marx, we should always start with economic power, since it forms the base for the other two. In the final analysis, therefore, economics conditions politics and the significant or ideological factors at large in society.

Today, this insight of Marx's, which is fundamentally correct, has been enriched by the contributions of cultural anthropology and of feminist thought and ecology.

Culture is a specifically human fact that pervades all the forces constituting social life. By culture, we mean the ways and means by which human beings organize what they do, and think and conceptualize in symbolic forms, including the meanings they attribute to all their activities, for culture is present in the economy and all other elements of society.

Today we regard the real life process, which embraces all dimensions of human existence, as being at the base of any society, rather than productive relationships, as Marx held. The problems of the human species and of production have been discussed by women. Giving birth to and bringing up children, cooking, washing, and looking after invalids, cannot simply be included in categories of "production" or "work," like manufacturing nuts and bolts or toothbrushes. The category of "reproduction," important for Marx as defining capital and its logic of accumulation through time, cannot be seen as synonymous with human reproduction, with all that this involves in the way of family relationships, which influence economic procedures in accordance with a particular culture (some people, for instance, even to their disadvantage, will not deal with persons of a race, creed, or ideology different from their own). Marxist analysis has nothing to say about this category.

The same can be said of the category of "social class." In a society consisting of classes and no longer of orders, such as our own, the class category is essential for understanding social structure and conflicts of interest. To abandon it would mean impoverishing our understanding to the detriment of the interests of the weakest. The class struggle, therefore, by becoming sensitive to ecological and holistic interests, acquires a new style. Now not only the interests of a class, or even of society as a whole, are taken into account, but also the welfare of nature. Therefore the category of "class struggle" does not embrace the whole gamut of relevant phenomena. The "generations" category is also important, as are "cultural values," by means of which major human groups establish their relationships and resolve their conflicts.

Marx saw the "industrial proletariat" as the bearer of class revolutionary consciousness and as the main creator of the new socialist society. Today there is a growing consensus that a variable hegemony is maintained instead by a conglomeration of forces, by the so-called popular classes, a term that comprises the historical and societal bloc of all those oppressed by the present order. This linked agglomeration of forces would be the historical agent of social change.

Ecological reflection has enriched certain aspects of the Marxist paradigm, so that some analysts speak of a second critique of political economy, one incorporating nature not as extrinsic, but intrinsic to the whole production process and as part of the forces of production. Nature is powerfully involved alongside labor in the accumulation of capital. Ecological awareness invites us to distance ourselves to a considerable degree from Marxist optimism on the "development of the forces of production." According to the laws of thermodynamics, for example, in order to function, productive forces must produce a quantity of energy that is consumed and can no longer be transformed into production or labor. Dialectically, therefore, there is no adequate way of distinguishing between destructive and constructive forces of production. This leads us to prefer renewable to nonrenewable energy sources, while simultaneously renouncing growth beyond certain limits.

In this overall context of positive critiques, of confirmation of the course and indication of the limits of Marxist social theory, the problem arises of the marginalized proletariat (the *Lumpen*), who loom so large on the vast periphery of the capitalist camp. In our dependent and associate capitalist societies, these make up the overwhelming majorities. They have been granted the vote and certain benefits of the populist state, but, living as they do at a mere subsistence level, they have no revolutionary potential. Their problem is not to transform society (which requires an awakened consciousness, a more or less defined strategy, and organizational tactics), but to ensure minimal subsistence levels for themselves. Conditioned in this way, they are easily manipulated by the representatives of the capitalist order. They promise immediate benefits, yet without modifying the situation of exclusion and dependence of the majority, for that would involve a transformation of society that would take it out of capitalist control.

Commentators are divided about how to interpret the breakthrough of these "wretched of the earth" onto the political scene, and about the pedagogy that would enable them to face up to the problems posed by their lives. The process known as *conscientization* is undoubtedly valid, but its ability to reach the masses is clearly limited. Is it possible to raise the consciousness of the masses? If they were made truly aware of their situation, they would no longer be a mass but an organized people. Conscientization is not only a pedagogical strategy but a value and a right appertaining to every human being. As such, however, it contains a strong dose of utopia, which cannot always be translated into practice. Fascist regimes knew how to address the consciousness of the masses, but influenced it in ways that did not correspond to the objective interests of the majority. The conservative wing of the Roman Catholic Church (like other popular churches of a Pentecostalist tendency) has always known how to steer the masses, by making clever use of effective symbols and significant archetypes. Its purpose has generally been to keep them in their sub-human state, by recourse to their capacities to sublimate, accept, and spiritualize the contradictions of that state.

We may ask: How do the masses, simply by virtue of their nature as mass, constitute an element that can hardly be conscientized and that, as a result, is destined to be led, like flood waters that have to find the lowest level in order to escape? The problem is to guide them in the direction of their real interests, which always lead in two basic directions: first, that of assuring a minimal standard of living, to enable material life to continue; second, of providing a definition of the ultimate meaning of the world and of life, once people reach the point at which they naturally ask themselves these questions. Guiding them within such parameters would not be tantamount to manipulating them in the interests of others, but would be pointing them in the right direction (in Latin, the word would be *manductio*, "leading by the hand"), to the benefit of the proletariat itself. The ruling group has a duty to stay in touch with the masses and never to lose an ethical sense of disinterested service.

Seen from the standpoint of faith, these marginalized people are those favored by God, the first heirs of the kingdom. If they cannot be agents of their own human history, they are nevertheless the natural citizens of the kingdom of the Son, who, by assuming human flesh, identified with them, and took up their cause. This view from the standpoint of faith enables us to consider the *Lumpen* in a particular way. They are no longer seen as political zeros because of their minimal revolutionary potential, since politics, ultimately, is not the sum total of human activity. They are rather those who emerge from the great ordeal and bear the seal of the Lamb in their flesh (see Rev 7:14). They are sacraments manifesting the presence of the Suffering Servant who, together with them, invokes the resurrection in which law and justice for all will be established on earth. In the base Christian communities, such people are changing themselves from a mass into a people, and through faith are becoming the people of God.

Liberation theology does not feel responsible, on the basis of its initial intuition, for the collapse of socialism or the crisis in Marxist thought. Marx was neither the father nor the godfather of liberation theology. This theology never opted for Marxism or for socialism; its option was for the poor. It saw socialism as a means of improving the lives of and of achieving greater justice for the oppressed. Liberation theology, as I have said above, lives by its original insight: the discovery of the intimate relationship between the God of life, the poor, and liberation. On this basis it has established a spirituality, a pastoral practice, and a theology. It is beneficial for the poor and for all the churches.

Marxism, enriched by cultural, ecological, and feminist analysis, is still an instrument in the hands of the oppressed for overturning the mechanisms that produce their poverty. The aspect of the truth that Marxism perceived in the past will always be true, for the conditions of destitution have not changed. Surely we must differ from the sophists, who produced a new truth for each client.

The truth of capitalist exploitation can be seen in the deteriorated social fabric of the rich nations and in the miserable lives of workers and unemployed of the nations on the periphery. The collapse of authoritarian socialism does not absolve capitalism of its sins and inherent perversion, which must always be denounced, especially now when it feels so euphoric and triumphant.

The Possibility of a Revolutionary Christianity

Christians in Nicaragua made a twofold contribution: one both practical and theoretical. In practice they helped, for evangelical reasons, to make the revolution against one of the most oppressive regimes in the history of Latin America. Then they comprised a significant force in consolidating the new order (the socialist Sandinista order), especially in the areas of health, education, and culture.

In theory they showed that it was possible to break the centuries-long stranglehold that the capitalist order had kept on Christianity. They also showed that a revolutionary Christianity was possible, not for opportunistic or political reasons, but as something intrinsic to the gospel itself. The gospel, in fact, when it transmits the subversive memory of Jesus of Nazareth, who personally chose the poor, is always revolutionary. It forces us to look at history from the underside, since this was Jesus' own viewpoint. It compels us to build history starting with the last, the victims of our social structures. Christians in Nicaragua showed all this in theory and in practice.

They made an inestimable contribution to world Christianity, unblocking preconceptions hostile to the idea of revolution and ushering in practices of liberation. The fact that they then lost the election is a political event, with understandable political reasons. The people did not vote against the revolution but for the end of a dirty war and for peace.

The challenge to which the Christians of Nicaragua responded still faces all Christians who live on the periphery of the capitalist empire. It is the challenge to make faith a form of protest, of resistance, of mobilization, and of liberation of the oppressed. It is these things as a result of Christian faith and the practice of Jesus, understood in their historico-social setting, and not as opportunistic applications of Jesus' faith and practice for the benefit of specific Christian or non-Christian interest groups.

In 1612 Felipe Guaman Poma de Ayala, a Peruvian Indian descended from the Incas, after living in Spain for thirty years, returned to Peru and for another thirty years lived in voluntary poverty, dedicated to seeking out "the poor of Jesus Christ." Very often, faced with the misery in which he found his brothers and sisters living, his indignation erupted in prayer: "My God, where are you? You are not listening to me in order to succor your people, whom I cannot succeed in helping." He, a layman, an Indian, and poor, set an example that has still not been followed by the church in Latin America. From an Indian viewpoint he saw a conformist Christianity, brimful of people yearning for liberation. God's call is heard through the cry of the oppressed of Latin America. Here it is not a question of socialism or of capitalism, but of obedience to the Word calling us to greater efforts to transform society.

This is the Word addressed to the churches. They can work with other groups to redeem the wretched of the earth, to safeguard creation, and to build a freedom that the world has not yet seen as it should be seen today. This is social and personal freedom, freedom in solidarity, freedom that shows compassion for those afflicted and for the troubles of their lives, and freedom to increase the freedom of others, to love the universe and all that is in it, with a strong and tender affection.

CHAPTER 6

Science, Technology, Power, and Liberation Theology

Liberation theology represents the mind of the parts of the church that have adopted the people's struggle so that they can make sure that society changes sufficiently to satisfy fundamental needs and allow the exercise of basic human rights. It arose, and continually arises, from the confrontation of human misery with the gospel, and of collective injustice with a thirst for justice; and it starts from a definite practice of liberation focused on the poor themselves as subjects of change.

The Dependent Capitalist System and Unsatisfied Needs

The specific and cruel experience of organized popular groups from the 1960s onward, which has been shared by many Christians (including bishops, priests, theologians, and pastoral workers), is that the thrust of the present socio-economic system has hindered (as it continues to hinder) the satisfaction of basic needs and respect for the person, and the social rights of the vast majority of the population.

Development may follow one of three models: that of an alliance between the bourgeoisie of a certain country with its people (populism); that of a pact between national groups and multinational trusts (alliance for progress); or, more recently, that of a modern, transnational, and populist neo-liberal state (modernization). In each case it takes place at the cost of an increasing impoverishment of the masses. If they are part of the system, they are exploited by it; if not, they are excluded from it.

In Latin America today the most crucial problem is not that of the poor within the dominant system, but that of the 30 to 40 percent of the population, the mass of the urban proletariat, who are excluded from it. They count for nothing economically, for their production and consumption are marginal in GNP terms. They do count politically, for they can vote and decide the outcome of elections, as happened recently in Argentina, Peru, Brazil, and Mexico. They vote for the candidates who speak to their profound awareness, and who can articulate fundamental deficiencies with the myth of a great father (with the characteristics of a protective mother), or of a hero, the savior of his country, who can give them bread, a roof over their heads, health care, and leisure. That is how the new populism is born; it manipulates these desires cleverly, but its ability to put them into effect is weak.

The non-satisfaction of basic needs is seen as oppression. It not only seems unlikely but has been shown to be impossible for the present socio-economic system applied in the Third World to satisfy the fundamental demands for life—and ongoing life—of most of the population.

Experience shows that within the dependent liberal-capitalist system (the capitalism, that is, of the Third World, of former colonies), there is no salvation for the poor, no respect for basic rights, and no satisfaction of basic needs. Therefore we have to abandon this system. The alternative may not be clear, but there is irrefutable evidence that we can expect no solution within the logic of capitalism for wage-earners or for those excluded from the system.

The pope's recent statement in *Centesimus annus* that the alternative to capitalism in the Third World should be sought not in socialism but in an improved form of capitalism (no. 42) has dashed the hopes of the oppressed. With the papal blessing, capitalists can now calmly condemn the poor of the world to another hundred years (*centesimus annus!*) of blood, sweat, and tears. The papal magisterium has never been so far from the truth and from compassion with the wretched of the earth.

The iron logic that constitutes the secret power of capitalism is that of the greatest profit in the shortest possible time. Any business that does not observe this law runs the risk of failing in competition with those that do. This logic can soften only if the stability of the market is guaranteed, or under exceptional circumstances, such as temporary collaboration to bring down the rate of inflation. Today, with continental economies and a global market, this law remains in force; it is absolutely necessary to observe it. Those who are not successful in the marketplace go under. What is not in the marketplace does not exist.

Faced with this bleak prospect for the poor, we seek liberation. Liberation is real only if political conditions for exercising justice are created. Social justice presupposes power and a different quality in its exercise. We therefore seek power for the people in order to obtain social justice and to satisfy people's basic needs efficiently and effectively. Otherwise, what freedom can we achieve for society as a whole?

Popular Power to Satisfy Needs and Ensure Freedom

Liberation theology locates science and technology within the triangle formed by the satisfaction of basic needs, justice for society, and power. In other words, it seeks power for the people, so that it can guarantee that basic needs are satisfied and that justice is obtained for society as a whole.

Consequently, science and technology are seen not as neutral elements standing alone (instrumental rationalization), but as dependent on the way in which society, politics, economics, and culture are organized. From the viewpoint of the poor of the Third World, science and technology today are the new caravelles, the main weapons for upholding political dependence and ensuring economic dominance over nations and their populations that do not control the production, distribution, and sale of goods. This statement does not amount to a rejection of science and technology. We need them to satisfy present-day basic human needs on a global scale. But we want to see them politically integrated in a society that sets itself better goals than unlimited growth (with the ecological violence this entails) and the greatest profit in the shortest time (leading to the marginalization and exclusion of the masses).

Liberation theology is in communion with the political aspirations of many social groups that seek a society concentrated on the dignity of the human person and on a form of participation that, through labor, satisfies the basic needs of food, shelter, health, education, and leisure, and opens up areas of freedom for creativity and the collective building up of society. Because of this, liberation theology is opposed to the technological messianism (the gospel of technocracy) of the ruling system. This claims to resolve the problems of underdevelopment, and its failed solution, which produced libertarian thinking in politics and in the churches. It seeks to do this by making intensive use of science and technology to produce food and everything else necessary for human sustenance, and by distributing them to those who are without them. Biotechnology has set itself such a goal.

This is the providentialist and assistentialist solution on a world scale. It is an agenda for guaranteeing survival (by providing food), but not for promoting life (by creating conditions for people to produce their food). Liberation theology is opposed to this kind of erroneous good will.

Technological Messianism Versus Participatory Politics

The problem cannot be reduced to guaranteeing survival, as though human beings were simply hungry animals (beings full of needs). Instead, it supposes an adequate vision of what human life is (human beings are beings made for freedom, for solidarity, for unlimited relationships, and with a capacity for communication, even with God). The logic of human life does not merely obey the instinct to reproduce, but seeks the advancement and expansion of systems of life. This logic is built on freedom, participation, communication, and creativity.

It is not enough, therefore, to distribute bread, which can be done by technological messianism. If we want to respect human nature, we have to create the appropriate conditions for producing food. That is, we have to provide work by means of participatory politics. Through work and the creativity it involves, human beings share in food production, build their houses, take care of their health, advance their education, organize their free time, and create conditions for communicating and expressing their world. They do not want to be simply creatures helped by the decisions of others, in a history made by others. They want to share in decision making and in a history which they themselves have helped to shape. That is, they want to construct their own individualities and their collective subjectivity. Only thus will they feel human and build up their own historical, ecological, and social humanity.

Finally, liberation theology seeks to throw light on society's agenda. In doing so it reflects on the power expressed through science and technology, which is deeply problematical. In effect, it is exercised with a capitalist agenda that produces a bad quality of life, both in the so-called First World and in the world in which two-thirds of the population live in poverty. The current process of globalization is being pursued within the capitalist ambit, yet not by means of religion, ethics, or ideology, but through the global market (in general, the needs of the market are not those of human beings).

Left to its own devices, the market eventually puts a price on everything and sets aside everything that is not profitable. Therefore, even if the great trusts, with their masses of technicians and technostructures, were to succeed in satisfying basic needs, the question of the nature of human beings, their freedom, creativity, sharing, and the meaning of their lives, which goes well beyond material needs, would remain unanswered.

Requisites of a New Global Political Economy

Liberation theology insists on this orientation: Technological globalization should be directed toward a worldwide political agenda (a new political economy), including a minimum of humanization, citizenship, equity, human, and ecological welfare, and respect for cultural differences and openness to cultural reciprocity and complementarity. I shall examine each of these elements briefly.

A minimum of humanization. All human beings should have the basic right to existence. This means that they should be able to eat at least one a meal a day, have a roof over their heads, and be helped with basic health care. Present regimes do not focus on whole persons, but only on their work effort (muscles, brains, the athlete's feet, and so on). It is revolutionary nowadays to say that we have to nourish love and friendship for human persons as such, beyond their ethnic, religious, or cultural attributes. The novelty of human rights movements in the Third World consists in reclaiming them primarily for the victims, and in taking as their motto: "Serve life, beginning with the most threatened."

Citizenship. Social systems should not tend to exclude people. All people should feel themselves to be potentially citizens of the world, used to thinking globally while acting locally in their own countries (with their own cultural roots). Citizenship implies anti-authoritarianism and the intrinsic acceptance of plurality.

Equity. This implies the certainty of being able to enjoy social benefits and of being able to overcome an established relationship between the contribution which certain citizens can make and what they receive in exchange. Equity seeks a greater realization of the political ideal of equality, which becomes a utopian goal in the positive sense of the term (a reference that makes relative all embodiments and continually invokes new ones). Solidarity among groups and nations alleviates the harshness of social inequalities.

Human and ecological welfare. The best projects, practices, and organizations are those that do not aim exclusively at the quality of goods and services, but at the quality of life, in order to make that life truly human. Society as a whole should make a life of this kind its goal. The alliance that is in the course of establishment between men and women and nature, in terms of brother-sisterhood and veneration, also forms part of human well-being. Another component is spirituality, in the sense of the capacity to communicate with the deepest subjectivity of other persons, and all other entities, including the otherness of all created beings and the absolute Otherness of God. Another, final, component is the pluralist expression of the values and visions of life, of history, and the ultimate goals and confines of the universe.

Respect for cultural differences. Human beings live in history. They have worked out their responses to the meaningful questions about their passage here on earth in different ways. Just as we have an external archeology (environmental and social ecology), so we have an internal ecology (profound ecology). We interpret, evaluate, and dream our existence on the basis of our cumulative experience. All this diversity reveals the richness of the venture and adventure that being human is. We have been able to communicate this, to the enrichment of all. In spite of the tendency of science and technology to homogenize everything, new singularities are constantly emerging from specific cultural appropriations of such processes. Each culture has a different way of expressing solidarity, of celebrating, of combining work and leisure, and of articulating great dreams with harsh reality. Science and technology are stages in this mode of inhabiting the earth and experiencing our integration in a greater ecological whole.

Cultural reciprocity and complementarity. It is not sufficient to recognize otherness. This act of respect is truly fulfilled when we accept the values of others, develop reciprocity (the exchange of experience and understanding), and reciprocally complement others. No one culture expresses the entire human creative potential. This means that one culture can complement another. All cultures together demonstrate the versatility of human beings and our various ways of fulfilling our humanity. In this way, every culture proffers an inestimable richness of language, philosophy, religion, and arts, as well as techniques and technologies—a whole way of living in the world. This is true whether we speak of a simple culture, such as that of the Amazonian tribes, or the "modern" scientific-technological form of culture.

In conclusion, liberation theology sees science, technology, and power as part of the program of redemption, construction, consolidation, and expansion of human life and freedom, starting with those who have the least life and freedom. Life and freedom are the greatest and most desirable goods in existence, without which we always feel enslaved to needs, but with which we can feel that we are sons and daughters of happiness.

CHAPTER 7

Theology of a Minor Liberation

A Personal Odyssey

Liberation theology has undergone a process of increasing refinement. It started in the 1960s by examining the most profound division in Latin American society, that between poverty and riches, and between exploitation and accumulation. This injustice cries out for criticism and for the overthrow of a social system that continually produces and reproduces this appalling dualism. Those who are to carry out this transformation would be the exploited popular classes themselves, organized among themselves and bearing a democratic agenda at grassroots level—the Latin American expression of the socialist utopia. But forms of oppression have many faces. We have become aware of cultural and ethnic oppression. The "witness cultures" of Latin America (Inca, Maya, Quechua, Aymara, Tupi-Guarani, and others) have been violently subjugated and, to a considerable extent, destroyed. Only by the grace of God have they survived today to denounce the oppression they have suffered and to rebuild the structures they have preserved in spite of this oppression.

Taking this into account, we are working out a theology of culture, a theology of liberationist stamp that has little to do with the culturalist and populist theologies developed in some parts of this continent. The understanding of racial oppression, especially of blacks, has also developed. This is one of the most cruel forms of oppression in our society. The blacks were reduced to slavery and still bear the scars. They have always been regarded as objects, as human fuel in the production of sugar, tobacco, and coffee. The ruling classes still consider the blacks as not fully human, and therefore as liable to be treated with violence and discrimination. At present the United States and other places are developing a powerful and prophetic black theology of liberation aimed at recovering the dignity of the black race, the legitimacy of its culture, and the worth of its religions.

The Global Need for Liberation

Another type of oppression that has now won recognition is sexual oppression, the oppression of women, who have been subjected for centuries to male domination in virtually all dominant cultures. Latin American culture and the ways in which we perceive reality, including the religious outlook, are macho, and thus lead to the marginalization of women. The result of this current of thought and the corresponding liberating practice is a vigorous feminist theology that allows everyone, men and women, to be more fully human. Reflection has also turned to other forms of oppression requiring liberation: of the handicapped, the old, children, the unemployed, drug addicts, homosexuals, and AIDS victims.

Each particular oppression requires a specific liberation. Yet the basic oppression, that of the socio-economically poor, has not been lost to sight. The others are always derivations of this fundamental form of oppression. Socio-economic oppression produces the class struggle (condemned by God and not willed by Christians in spite of its brutal efficacy). Here groups demonstrate their antagonism and their irreconcilable interests, whereas women's, blacks', and Indians' struggles concern groups not naturally antagonistic to one another. Their basic interests are, in principle, reconcilable. Blacks can be reconciled to Latinos, Indians to technologists, and women to men; the exploited worker can never be reconciled to the exploiting boss. This socio-economic oppression makes the others worse: blacks, Indians, and women are doubly oppressed when they are both poor and isolated.

These various forms of oppression, referred back to one basic but not exclusive type, the socio-economic kind, demand a process of liberation that will lead to a new type of relationship in production, political structures, and the creation of value. This is the great agenda, political and utopian in character, underlying all the struggles of the oppressed. They are the bearers of this new hope, the basic agents of changes supported by allies who have taken up their cause, struggle, and destiny. The various expressions of liberation theology are to be found hard at work, interacting with one another, in this context.

A Militant Presence on the Side of the Deprived

There is yet another final and profound level of liberation theology, emphatically present in those who fight daily on the side of the oppressed and wretched. Liberation theology imposes on theologians the demand to struggle boldly and unstintingly on the side of the people. As they fight their way deeper into the world of the oppressed, they discover a new universe, a new culture, and a new hope, or an extreme form of despair.

At this level theologians become ever more profoundly committed. It is not their words or minds that are needed but their hearts and hands. Here, we have truly reached the deepest level. Beyond this there is only death. The basic agenda is survival: to guarantee the minimum of food, once a day. How and where to hide to get through the night and safeguard one's meager personal possessions. How to prevent chronically sick children from dying. How to ensure some minimal contact between husband and wife, children and parents.

Here we are not dealing with the great sweep of liberation, with economic structures, political alternatives, alliances and interaction with other liberation fronts. On the objective level, indeed, all this is necessary and, to be sure, indispensable if we are to transform the situation of wretchedness. But the intensity of oppression and the brutalization deriving from the struggle for survival prevent us from posing these problems in subjective terms. We have to move to the second level, that of a full plate, a ready bed, and a reliable means of transport.

In these circumstances we see the iniquity of poverty. It is a sin that God can never wish. It is so perverse that it affects people in their inner depth, forcing them back on themselves (because it is a question of biological survival), envious, embittered, and lacking in the desires introjected in them by capitalist domination. People curse God. They corrupt their human, sexual, and economic relationships. Then theologians begin to think: If God exists, God is on their side; if God does not exist, we need to invent God to give an ultimate meaning to these suffering servants, victims of the social system, to revindicate a final justice, and to rebuild their lives.

Favorite Daughters and Sons

If heaven is not for those who on earth have known only hell, then I do not want to go to the heaven of the God of good moralists. That God would be one without a heart. How could one live forever with a God who has no heart? These who are condemned on earth are condemned only on earth, while they are the beloved daughters and sons of God. They permanently embody the figure of the Suffering Servant. They are saved not because of their virtue, but because they share in the passion of the Son of God through their everyday passion. Their curses are supplications, pleasing to God and heard by God.

It is perhaps only because of them that salvation is continually mediated to the whole of humanity. Because of this salvation that is in them by the grace of God, from time to time there is an inrush of human actions that restore faith in God and hope in God's reign. A woman holds on her knees, as in a Pietà, her fifteen-year-old son, killed by the police. He was her only son, the one who scavenged for what they needed to live on in the city. She is in despair but cannot weep because she has no more tears. Her desolation is complete. I ask her: "Can you still believe in God?" She raises her eyes to me. They are unforgettably full of a tenderness so intense that it must be divine. She says: "How can I doubt God who is my Father? What can I cling to, if I do not cling to God and do not feel myself in God's hands?"

God is so real that not even the harshest misfortune can blot out faith. Marx was mistaken. On this most profound of all levels, faith is not an opium. It is a shining liberation. It is the light that pushes aside the darkness and guarantees life against death sought through desperation or death that supervenes from exhaustion. Such a situation enables us to understand the truth of Jesus' good news: "Blessed are you who are poor, for yours is the kingdom of God." The kingdom is yours because God is the God of life, of tenderness to those who are unjustly cut down. In spite of all your moral and social miseries, it is for you that there is the kingdom, where there is life, freedom, abundance of everything needed for life. Only in this way is the gospel good news. Otherwise it is a moral lesson like the lessons of the learned and of bigots. Only thus can it radically surpass the pharisaism of good deeds, of the God who loves only good people and does not love, as Luke says, "the ungrateful and the wicked" (6:35).

The Heaven of the Deprived

We have to realize that most churches have not learned this lesson. The condition for learning this good news is to immerse ourselves in the hell of the oppressed. There we shall find the heaven of the God of Jesus Christ, which is the only heaven worth looking for, because it includes all those we have cast out.

Theologians and pastoral workers who walk in the warren of the lives of the poor should be ready to divest themselves of everything. They will never be able to set their own schedule; they will have to be prepared to cut out leisure time, because the poor have no leisure and their problems take no account of our schedules. They will not leave off thinking, because thinking is an attitude of mind and an impulse of the spirit, but they will have to postpone their writing to an unknown future date. They feel called to live charity in all its breadth, rather than an understanding of faith in its theological formulation.

It is no matter of chance that liberation theologians write progressively less. Identification with the poor, taking up their lives and struggles, makes them companions in all critical moments. Quite often, when we have time to put our thoughts in order and in writing, we are so tired and inwardly wounded that we do not have the psychological or human inclination for a task like that.

This is possibly the moment of full liberation, when we are liberated from ourselves in order to be available to others as genuinely as possible. Then we shall speak less about liberation, but live its thrust together with the oppressed who survive and dream (for that is all that is left to them) of a full liberation. But that will come, for he who promised it demonstrated in his own self the full liberation of all who live.

PART 3

FROM WORLD CONSCIOUSNESS TO MYSTICISM

Globalization, or world-consciousness, is holistic by definition. Accordingly, the new eco-systemics cannot be restricted to technology, politics, and the nature of civil society, but must include the dimensions of ethics, mind, and spirit.

The new ethical order is not more anthropocentric but ecocentric, striving as it does to bring about the equilibrium of the entire cosmic community. But the new ethics needs a new mental basis to support it. Psychology has tried to understand that the world lies not so much before us as also (and perhaps primarily) behind, that is, inside us. The new way of looking at the world must come to birth within us if it is to be translated into external reality. Mental ecology tries to reconstruct the intimate thrust of humankind toward the correct valuation of, and appropriate entry into, the cosmos. The human mind and heart have a special place for those promptings of the spirit that urge humankind to a mystical relation with the universe as a whole. In this new conception, spirit is contrasted not with body but with death. To be spiritual means living in accordance with the thrust of life toward and in unison with society and nature. In its mature stage, spirituality becomes mysticism. This allows us to transcend the material limitations of things and to discern behind the structure of reality that "area" where tenderness comes into its own. It also shows us where the welcoming and loving mystery prevails that enables us to communicate with God, the Father and Mother whose loving kindness is boundless.

The present crisis of the church and of the major religions is essentially due to an agonizing deprivation: the lack of any profound experience of God. To be sure, in their remote corner of Planet Earth some believers have taken up the anguished protest of the dispossessed. They now follow a new path, that leading to the liberation of modern slaves. They move toward the new earth promised to those who—together with Francis of Assisi and so many others—acknowledge as brothers and sisters to love all creatures and all manner of things.

CHAPTER 8

Nurturing Our Mysticism

One of the most original phenomena in Latin-American society is the proliferation of social movements. By social movements I mean those groups founded to promote specific causes not supported by the state or recognized by organized society. Instead, such groups make it their business to ensure that the needs for which those causes stand are satisfied. In general, they are engaged in struggle for fundamental rights that have been violated or left unsatisfied. For instance, they join and support movements for human rights that view things from a social standpoint. Essentially, these movements demand satisfaction of the rights of the poor to life, work, and the minimal fulfillment of basic needs. They are movements of landless peasants, of homeless groups, of shanty-town dwellers, of women, of street urchins, and of blacks, Indians, and others. There are also quasi-political groups with popular programs for changing society: trade union cells, various social pastoral initiatives of the church (in respect to land, homes, health, and political participation; on behalf of blacks, Indians, and the poor), and various discussion and action groups.

The people who take part in such movements are militants, committed individuals who sacrifice some of their leisure time or sleep to investigate questions and to organize and fight for the rights denied them. These movements have to confront an unjust structure and the historical indifference of the ruling classes to social questions concerning the working classes. They come up against the cynicism of the well-to-do, who always find a thousand excuses to quash militant groups and guarantee their own political hegemony—and thus their privileges.

For centuries some groups, such as blacks and peasants, have tried to resist the process of domination and marginalization, but are scarcely organized. Other people, imbued with humanitarian and libertarian ideals, have created groups that are active politically and, sometimes, even organized along military lines to try to introduce by force the necessary but always historically delayed social change. All these groups testify to the dramatic, even tragic nature of the struggle, for they meet with one failure after the other. Their movements are threatened if not smashed by police repression or oligarchical power. The history of Latin America is largely written in blood and tears. Not all the victims are dead and buried, for repression is not yet at an end. Nevertheless, resistance has not been entirely vanquished and attempts at liberation still occur.

What secret power feeds these movements? Where do they find the hope that enables them to continue to dream, to resist, and to want a more humane and happier society for themselves and for their sons and daughters?

Our continent has always shown evidence of inspiration by the original Christian utopia and its dream of a society of brothers and sisters. This would be a just society in which all people would share; a society full of tender feeling for the poor and marginalized; a society aware of the social consequences of the fact that every human being is a child of God. There have always been those who, under the banner of that awareness, have pleaded for an end to the colonization of Indians and slaves, to the exploitation of labor, and to elitism. There are those now who opt for the poor and exercise their option at the basis of the church. They offer an appropriately contemporary version of the libertarian dimension of the subversive memory of Jesus of Nazareth.

Others take up the emancipatory ideals of the French Revolution, the ideals of liberty, equality, and fraternity. They try to put these principles into practice in spite of the opposition of inimically organized societies. People of this caliber are committed to spreading the notion of a participatory and popular democracy through discussion, by means of politically militant groups, and by joining so-called progressive parties.

For millions of people, socialism and communism have offered a current of generosity and have seemed an inspiring source of true love for the oppressed, of revolutionary visions, and of libertarian practice that can be applied wherever social reform is needed. In spite of the crisis of socialism "as it really is" (in other words, the kind of social and state organization that follows, say, the Leninist concept of the single-party state), the socialist idea has survived as a force for mobilizing social commitment. Socialism grows from a profound rejection of deprivation and suffering. It develops in acts of political and revolutionary love for the oppressed of a society marked by social inequality.

Radical humanism and an ethics of compassion and solidarity inspire other people to committed support of Indians, blacks, women, AIDS victims, the physically disadvantaged, and so many others penalized by a dominative society.

This process involves what we may term the mysticism of commitment and struggle. The number is constantly growing of those who locate themselves within a holistic and integral philosophy of human existence. In so doing, they try to disclose the various dimensions of the mystery of life and the various levels of human commitment. They identify themselves with the great dreams and visions of a new world and of human and social relations imbued more thoroughly with compassion and love that spark the imagination and stir the heart. In this context spirituality and God become truly meaningful in everyday events, in major decisions, in achievements, and in setbacks— in short, in the great drama of humankind and human history. They are especially significant when individuals and groups have to confront failure and defeat yet retain the courage and strength to resist, protest, commit themselves, and venture everything in a just cause. Where do they find this vital energy and enthusiasm?

I do not mention mysticism in order to avoid answering specific questions or to mystify reality. I use the concept to stress the more radiant aspect of things, the dimension that feeds vital energy and the principle of concern, as well as the power to continue through failure as well as success.

Spirituality and mysticism form part of life in its wholeness and in its sacredness. They support the thrust of resistance and the persistent longing for liberation.

Nature of Mysticism

The term *mysticism* is related to mystery. Mystery has many meanings; it can also be used pejoratively. In everyday usage the word *mystery* may be used of an idea beyond reason and to suggest intentions or a reality concealed from ordinary mortals. Mystery can also mean the atmosphere of interest, curiosity, and fascination surrounding a certain person.

Originally the word *mystery* (*mysterion* in Greek is derived from *myein*, which means "discerning the hidden, hitherto unspoken nature of a reality or an intention") was associated with religious experience gained through initiation rites. In these ceremonies, through celebrations, songs, dances, and the dramatization and practice of ritual gestures, an individual receives a revelation and a form of illumination reserved for a well-defined and chosen group. Mystery is connected with this actual experience, which has a universal frame of reference.

This is not a matter of listening to a catechism lesson about some esoteric and incomprehensible doctrine, or of being told about a vision of the ineffable, but of undergoing a communitarian religious experience. This kind of experiential process was called a mystery to indicate that it was imparted to a group of initiates undergoing a special course of preparation for its reception, and not merely to any curious spectator.

Only much later, in philosophical speculation, was mystery separated from experience. It came to be used not for the social and communitarian but for the rational aspect of a doctrine or revelation. One may speak therefore of the Christian mystery of the Trinity, of the incarnation, of grace, and so forth. But here we enter into what is properly theological reflection and not mystical experience. Of course these "mysteries," through the person professing them, can encourage an authentically mystical experience.

I shall now describe some positive aspects of mystery and mysticism, which will help the reader to grasp the nature of the force underlying militancy. My purpose is practical: to reinforce and deepen the understanding of the notion. I should like to explicate the concept in terms of present-day usage and to distinguish that from its usage in the past.

Existential Anthropological Significance of Mystery and Mysticism

Mystery is not an enigma which, once explained, disappears. Mystery is the dimension of depth to be found in every person, in every creature, and in reality as a whole; it has an necessarily unfathomable, that is, inexplicable aspect.

Various approaches (emotive, mythic, intuitive, scientific, and holistic) enable us to conceive of something, even the most material thing, from the infinitely small to the infinitely large. Whatever line we follow in considering something, we must also remember that there are always other aspects and viewpoints to take into account. If we really think of the infinitely complex nature of the human being, man and woman, we become clearly aware of the existential meaning, at an experiential level, of a mystery and begin to understand how we should see mysticism.

Every individual is a mystery. We may come to know him or her through long acquaintance, in the intimacy of love, by recourse to the sciences, or in the light of various human traditions. Yet, whatever concept or setting we choose, no one can really spell out in full the precise meaning of Mary, John, George, James, Sue, Ellen, or anyone else. Ultimately, to himself or herself, and to everyone else, an individual is a mystery, a secret. We know only what a person may freely reveal in the course of his or her life, what may be seen from without, and what may be gleaned from various forms of understanding that we have developed. Nevertheless, in spite of all this, the living, personal mystery of the individual always confronts us anew.

Mystery, however, does not constitute a reality to be contrasted with or set against knowing. It is part of the nature of mystery that it should be known. But it is also characteristic that it should continue to be mysterious even when known. That is the very paradox of mystery. It is not the end of reason but rather reason in its unrestricted aspect. It enables us to know reality not exhaustively, till there is no more to be known, but with the assurance that there is more to be known, that this more can be known better, and be known to the point of infinity.

In one sense, this process is, so to speak, an example of our modern scientific, experimental, and technological paradigm, which does not reveal all the dimensions of reality but only whatever can be apprehended in experimental dialogue with nature. But even then it is an infinite dialogue. There are also other forms of dialogue, because different cultures and various historical eras have developed a thousand forms of knowledge, whether through dreams, intuition, myth, and symbols, or through religious and philosophical thought and in other modes of apprehension.

What we call reality proves immeasurably greater than our reason and our will to dominate it by knowing; the human per-

son is something more than ways of knowing and forms of social cohabitation. The human individual is a mystery that discloses its meaning only under the most ambiguous guise. On
the one hand, a human being may seem quite tender, desirous
of communion and communication, longing to welcome and to
be welcomed. On the other hand, he or she may also reveal a
dark and terrifying side, indeed a capacity to destroy, exclude,
and behave like a wolf to humankind.

The organ best fitted to comprehend this mystery is the heart
and what Pascal called the *esprit de finesse*—intuition. This is
an attitude of basic sympathy, a fundamental ability to empa-
thize with others in their actual situation. We discern, or intuit,
their vulnerability. Other people show interest in us, and we
are able to indicate our concern for them, without any *esprit de
géometrie*—without, that is, calculation.

This understanding is existential. It is available to all. Moreover, eminent scientists such as Niels Bohr, Werner Heisenberg,
Max Planck, David Bohm, and Albert Einstein, among others,
testify to the experience of mystery. In *The World As I See It*
(1938) Einstein wrote that he was most powerfully moved by
the mystery of life. It was the same feeling that awakened beauty
and truth, and created art and science, the hidden reality of
mystery. Einstein said that perceiving mystery was of fundamental importance for the creative scientist, for it brought
to awareness all those dimensions that were inaccessible to
scientific formulas and enabled the scientist to remain basically humble. He stated emphatically that cosmic religion
was the most weighty and powerful inspiration of scientific
research and that the scientific spirit could not exist without it.

We are not confronted with a new doctrine or ideology but
with a basic experience of reality in the aspect of things. This
experience, which is inaccessible to analytical reason, does not
confront us with some new doctrine or ideology, but with reality experienced in its essential, indeed fundamental, aspect.
Cold reason does not evoke that attitude to reality which is

compounded of veneration, delight, and humility, and which, as a reaction to mystery glimpsed in its utter profundity, we may justly term mystery.

Science expounds rational things rationally, just as they are, by stating how they are. But the actual truth of a thing's existence, what its mystery truly amounts to, cannot be enunciated in this way. We must rejoice, we must lose ourselves in wonder, at the mystery of existence. An authentic approach to mystery has to be mystical and contemplative.

Claude Lévi-Strauss, the famous anthropologist who worked for many years in Brazil and among the Indians, once gave an account of his intellectual life. He said of his faith in scientific knowledge that he was fascinated by everything that he taught in physics and biology. At the same time, when solving a particular problem, he found that it always gave rise to a new one, and so on to infinity. The result was ever and again to bolster his conviction that the true nature of reality must always elude any attempt to represent it appropriately.

Reality is one thing, but the image that we make of it is another. This is always the case. We never "catch up with" reality itself. The real nature of mystery always evades our attempts to conceptualize it, and escapes the nets of our language and symbolism. Its depths are never plumbed. Mystery is always linked to passion, enthusiasm, and all great emotions, in short to life's deepest and greatest impulses. Alceu Amoroso Lima, one of the leading Christian intellectuals of twentieth-century Brazil, said in his last book, *Everything Is Mystery* (*Tudo é Mistério* [Petrópolis, 1983]), that mystery was at the root, in the trunk, in the flower, and in the fruit of everything, and that its cultivation was the royal road to truth.

Once we begin effectively to espy the mysterious, we see the most impeccably traditional doctrines waver, the most precise formulations fade to nothingness, and the most profound symbols dissolve. If we are open to mystery at the beginning and at the end of our inquiries we shall eventually discover a more replete, human, and personal form of truth.

To nurture mystery at this level means keeping a lively and open curiosity about reality and developing a new awareness of the limits of our knowledge. It means always beginning anew in the face of the untold richness of experience, and always being ready to draw on any source of wisdom and from different cultural traditions. It also means continuing humbly to venerate and remaining enthusiastic before the astonishingly various aspects of reality which, though utterly beguiling, must always elude our most subtly devised attempts to represent it. This mystical approach is available to all of us without exception, as long as we are human and remain aware.

The Religious Significance of Mystery and Mysticism

When an individual becomes personally aware of the experience of mystery, it is as if he or she had received an invitation to dialogue and prayer and had been asked to bow down to something entirely sacred. In other words, mystery demands a quasi-religious attitude, and in fact an experience of mystery is at the root of all religions.

Those who experience mystery are mystics. The experience of mystery is not only a matter of ecstasy. It is also an everyday affair of experiencing wonder at the sacred aspect of reality and of life. We all feel this kind of wonder, of ecstasy, before a newborn child. Other, similar forms of the sacred demand our respect. Surely we also feel a similarly deep and solemn respect at the hollow, suffering countenance of a Bolivian highlander? Who is not rendered speechless by the heavy, calloused feet of a north-eastern peasant working from dawn to dusk in parched land far from any village?

Mysticism is not the privilege of the fortunate few. It is rather a dimension of human life to which all of us have access when we become conscious of a deeper level of the self, when we try to study the other side of things, when we become aware of the inward richness of the other, and when we confront the grandeur, complexity, and harmony of the universe. All of us, at a certain level, are mystics.

Mystics use appropriate words to describe mystery, but it is a presumptuous and daring task, for mystery is the unnameable. We call it God, Atman, Tao, Yahweh, El, Father, and so on. The name is not important. It will always be a kind of label for what is nameless. In regards to this experience of ascribing a name to the unnameable, in the first century C.E. the Chinese sage Chuang-Tzu wrote: "The Tao is a name which indicates without defining. The Tao is beyond words and things. It can be expressed neither with words nor with silence. Where there are neither words nor even silence, Tao is perceived" (*The Way of Chuang Tzu*).

First of all comes the experience of mystery, the experience of God. Only afterward does faith supervene. Faith is not primarily adhesion to a teaching that gives access to revelation and the supernatural. Then faith would be tantamount to ideology, in the sense of an idea or belief inculcated in someone from outside. This extrinsic character of so-called faith can give rise to various forms of fundamentalism and religious warfare. All groups tend to affirm their own truths to the exclusion of all others.

Faith is meaningful and possesses truth only when it represents a response to an experience of God made personally and communally. Then faith is the expression of an encounter with God which embraces all existence and feeling—the heart, the intellect, and the will. The occasions and times of such encounters become sacraments, points of reference to a form of experience that is overwhelmingly, irrefutably significant. Jacob gave a name to the place where he met God. He called it Penuel, for as he said, "I have seen God face to face" (Gen 32:31). Theology emerges from this kind of experience. It represents an attempt to translate a fundamental experience into terms proper to reason (doctrine), practice (ethics), and celebration (liturgy). The very names given to God originate in a primordial experience. Yahweh, for example, means the accompanying God, present in the life of the people; Elohim means the God who illumines the way and shines forth into existence.

The present crisis in the church and in the historical religions consists in the painful absence of a profound experience of God. Church offices are occupied by hierarchs, by crusading missionaries, and by doctrinal experts, in other words, by religious power. They are not interested so much in the truth of God as in the security of their religious system.

Those who testify to something more are the mystics, the faithful who bear witness to God and, in God's name, without permission from anyone, inaugurate a new form of discourse and introduce new types of behavior.

Religions crystallize as a consequence of religious experience. Their institutions are valuable in that they preserve that experience, transmit it to successive generations, and arrange things so that individuals are inspired to become religious.

The truly religious individual, much more than some priest-guardian of sacred wisdom about God, possesses a mystical form of knowledge. This is an experiential knowledge imbued with the evidence of encounters with God. Such encounters help to reinvigorate religious institutions. Then enthusiasm is preserved and energy is found to struggle and to predict an era of greater justice, in spite of the church and of other official religions.

The Christian Significance of Mystery and Mysticism

Judaism and Christianity identify mystery and God in the history of the people, above all in the history of the oppressed. They profess a historical God, the God of Abraham, of Isaac, and of Jacob; the God of the prophets; and, in Christianity, the God of Jesus of Nazareth. The God of history is presented as an ethical God. Accordingly, the mysticism of the Bible is a mysticism of open eyes and of active hands. The follower and servant of God is the one committed to justice; the one who stands up for the weak; and the one brave enough to denounce a purely celebratory religion without the mediation of neighborly love.

Israel experiences God in the struggle of the oppressed in captivity in Egypt and of those deported to Babylon. God is said to hear the cries of the oppressed, leave the inaccessible light, and promise to rescue the people from affliction and injustice (Ex 3; 4). Those who feel abandoned, the orphans and pilgrim people, must see that their ways are the ways of God and that the Lord pleads their cause (cf. Dt 10; Jer 22:15; Prv 22:22-23), for, when they are deserted and no one succors them, God will help them. It is said that "he who oppresses a poor man insults his Maker, but he who is kind to the needy honors him" (Prv 14:31). The Messiah's mission is one of liberation; it is to offer justice to the abandoned and to plan the inauguration of a new order of peace, brotherhood and sisterhood, in view of the ultimate reign of divine law and justice (cf. Is 11:4-9; 42:1-4).

This mystique of ethical commitment—because God is to be found in just actions and in loving relations with others—is accompanied by a mystique of contemplation. The entire universe was created by God. Human beings are representatives of God; men and women are divine agents in their being and in their action. We observe the signs of God's hand in everything: in all created things and in the spiritual and physical reality of humankind. The praise and exaltation of a fervent soul accords with this experience of God in the works of creation and in human efforts.

The Christian scriptures extend and radicalize the same line of experience of God in history. It testifies that God whole and entire has entered into human reality and has taken human form in Jesus of Nazareth. Henceforth the preferred place for encounters with God will be human life and, in particular, the life of the Crucified. This God is not incarnate in Caesar on his throne, or in priests at the altar, but in the image of the oppressed and the excluded who are sent outside the city to be crucified. The transcendent mystery in incarnate form is revealed as the crucified Jesus. The prayer of the cross is for life and resurrection.

The resurrection of the crucified Jesus is a sign of reaffirmation of the primacy of justice and of life. It states that insurrection against the order of this world is sacred and reveals the universal promise that those who have been unjustly oppressed will inherit the fullness of life, which is resurrection. Jesus makes himself one of the oppressed. His fortunate destiny is promised to all those who suffer a similar fate.

Christian mysticism, being historical, accords with Jesus. It implies a commitment to solidarity with the poor, for Jesus wishes to be one of them. He personally gathers up the marginalized from the country roads and from city squares and streets. Christian mysticism implies a commitment to personal and social change, and to the utopia, preached by Jesus, of the kingdom of God. That utopia will inaugurate its era of fulfillment in justice for the poor and, thereafter, for all people and for all creation.

Following Jesus, because of the new proposals which he makes, creates conflict. Because of those ideas some people will resort to symbolic or physical violence. Therefore following Jesus may mean persecution and in the end martyrdom. But everything is accepted joyfully as the price that has to be paid for solidarity with the suffering people and with the suffering servant Jesus. In the suffering of the poor and the marginalized a Christian perceives the presence and enactment of the suffering of Jesus, which is repeated in the flesh and reverberates in the cries of his brothers and sisters. Moreover, in the progress made toward the establishment of justice and the promotion of life, we may see factual and historical signs of resurrection.

There is another clearly contemplative, mystical aspect found in the Christian scriptures. It affirms that both the incarnate Son and the Spirit are concerned with the mystery of creation. They are present in it like ferment in the process of ascension toward the reign of the Trinity. We may say that the universe shares in the blessings conferred on humankind. It participates in the resurrection of all flesh. There is a future for the stars, for the mountains, for plants, for animals, and for people. Faith is adamant about this but is silent about the contours of the ultimate kingdom and life within it.

Their assurance of the general resurrection in this sense enabled the early Christians to speak of the cosmic Christ and of the Spirit's dwelling in the energy of the universe and of life. This omnipresence of Christ and the Spirit was a favorite notion of St. Francis of Assisi, who saw all created things and beings, from the sun and the moon to birds and snails, as sacraments of God and as brothers and sisters. Teilhard de Chardin updated this experience in the context of modern cosmology and tried to identify the emergence of consciousness and the unequivocal sign of God's presence in the movement of matter toward ever greater complexity. Cosmogenesis, which leads to anthropogenesis and then to Christogenesis, which in its turn gives way to theogenesis, ends in a state of ultimate fulfillment, the culmination of the entire process, when all things are gathered up in God.

The sequential mystique is historical; it leaves room for action. The Christian mystique, the mysticism of the spirit, is cosmic, open to the future. It seeks unity in all differences, searching for it as the divine thread that runs through the entire universe and all consciousness and human action, until it unites ahead and above in the prospect of supreme synthesis with God, the omega-point of evolution and creation. This mysticism of union and unity is clearly indebted to the powerful current which descends from the Greek Fathers (Gregory of Nyssa and Gregory of Nazianzus), passes down through the Platonic and Augustinian tradition, pauses at St. Bonaventure with his wonderful *Itinerarium Mentis ad Deum* (*Journey of the Soul to God*), and carries on only to culminate in St. John of the Cross (*Ascent to Mount Carmel*) and St. Teresa of Avila (*The Interior Castle*). It then flows out into Teilhard de Chardin's ardently mystical texts *The Divine Milieu* and *Science and Christ.*

In short, Christian mysticism has encouraged a gradual re-working and refinement of the image of God which is both trinitarian and replete with the notion of communion. God is not a figure of solitude but the communion of three divine fig-ures, the Father, the Son, and the Spirit. They are co-existent and dwell together eternally without any hierarchy among them-selves. They are distinct yet favor self-giving and communion among themselves. The interrelationship of life and love among them (*perichoresis*, in theological terminology) is so profound and radical that it is the means by which they are, so to speak, unified and constitute one God.

The Trinity is neither an absurd mystery nor a mathematical contradiction, but the supreme expression of the experience of love and human communion which we all undergo. In love it is important to be distinct and not to amalgamate. But it is essen-tial that the giving of one to the other should be such that no harm is done to the overall unity. It is not enough to have a *tête-à-tête*, as it were, of an "I" (the Father) and a "Thou" (the Son), for that would amount to dual narcissism. The "I" and the "Thou" have to meet in an "us" (the Holy Spirit), like a third person overcoming the isolation of two separate individu-als. Thus there is a perfect dialectic not merely of two but of three persons, who are distinct but always interrelated.

Accordingly, the Trinity is the utopian realization of some-thing hinted at in our own existence in the relationship among man, woman, and child. Or better, we are already aware of it in our own lives, for the vital passion of the divine Persons is already there; it is the ground of our life and present in the impulse that fires our capacity to love. It is the best possible community, the prototype of a society that welcomes differ-ence and creates union by means of communion among three different beings.

The mystery of the communion-life of the trinitarian God is not a product merely of the speculative power of early Christian thinkers. Discourse about the Trinity is the way in which Christ's disciples almost ingenuously and unreflectively translated into vivid terminology their experience of Jesus Christ the Nazarene. They knew him only as the Son. He related to God as his Father. So much charisma and so much attractive power shone forth that the Spirit's presence was evident. Accordingly, in Jesus we perceive the mystery as Father/Mother, as Son/Daughter, and as Spirit. The notion of the Trinity expressed this combined experience in the following sense: behind everything, behind all being, within all life, and in the thrust of all passion is a love and three lovers, a communion and three interrelated subjects. The Trinity is no multiple God but a revelation of the nature of the divine Mystery as communion and relationship.

Judeo-Christian mysticism, in spite of mediocre institutions and the spiritual indolence of most of those who profess it, does demonstrate its politico-liberational-contemplative character. It does not accept the world as it is. It wants to change and reconstruct it on the basis of sharing, solidarity, brotherhood and sisterhood, work, leisure time, and veneration for the mystery of creation. This kind of commitment allows one to feel like a servant of God in history, and an agent of God's policy in the world. This means that the kingdom will be inaugurated always and only where justice triumphs, collaboration is affirmed, the spirit of enmity is overcome, love is practiced, and everything proceeds, sweetly moving, sweetly singing, toward the supreme integration of all things, all creatures, through God and in God.

The Socio-political Significance of Mysticism

What is in fact mysticism, but sometimes comes closer to what is meant by its cognate term *mystique*, also appears in the discourse of social and political scientists. It is found in Max Weber or Pierre Bourdieu, and in others who analyze politics

as a profession and art and discuss the importance of the charismatic figures who help to change society. Mysticism in this
sense is a combination of deep convictions, noble visions, and
strong passions, which stir and spur people and movements to
show their will to struggle, or which inspire procedures capable of confronting this or that problem and of sustaining hope
in the face of historical setbacks.

Utopia is always active in politico-social mysticism. This is
the capacity of projecting, on the basis of the potentiality of
reality, new historical dreams, alternative models, and different projects. In general, the bearers of new visions are the oppressed groups, those who, even when defeated, do not
surrender but stoutly resist and always take up the struggle
again. They are inspired by dreams of a new reality, which remove the sense of fatality from history and do not restore as a
historical necessity the unjust situation imposed and maintained
by the force of oppression.

Society may be termed visionary if it is always looking ahead,
for there is always an anti-power opposed to the dominant
power. It is always there in a subversive form, always intent
upon combining liberators and organizations to ensure that the
transformation of society never ceases. All this is a form of
mysticism that refuses to accept the status quo, a mystique gen-
erating a form of energy directed to the construction of a better
future.

Logically, utopia as a whole will be realized in history and
will always liberate new energy to ensure that the way remains
open for it. At the same time, the utopian thrust will ensure
that all achievements are duly relative, so that history does not
stand still, congealing as it were in some reactionary mode, but
is always open to new progress and to further advances toward
utopia.

Mysticism, then, is the secret motor of all commitment, the
enthusiasm which continually powers the militant. It is the interior fire arousing the individual in spite of the monotony of
everyday tasks. It allows assurance and serenity to persist in

spite of equivocation and failure. This mysticism is a mystique that would sooner allow acceptance of defeat with honor than seek for a victory with shame, for such a victory would depend on a neglect of moral values and thus on manipulation and lies.

Mysticism and Militancy

There is no militancy without passion and without mystique, irrespective of the nature of the cause, whether it is religious, humanist, or political. The militant lives in the world for good things and values, for the sake of which time is spent, risks are run, and a life commitment is made. It is not so much a matter of having certain ideas as of living out convictions. It is a matter of changing praxis and thus of transforming social relations.

Ideas of themselves cannot change actual reality or history. History is preserved, reformed, or transformed to the extent that some social actors are fundamentally committed militants and fighters, in one direction or the other. The mystique that galvanizes social movements is of supreme importance for them.

To illustrate the link between mystique and militancy, I shall quote an example from the practice of many centers for the defense and protection of human rights, which are so important in Latin America, in view of the level and nature of oppression. These centers, constantly spied on, calumniated and persecuted, live by virtue of their supporters' irrepressible conviction that every individual is an equally entitled bearer of human dignity, irrespective of whether he or she is defined as boss or worker, black suffering from discrimination or white oppressor, victimized woman or macho man, bank robber or banker.

Every human being, man or woman, child or adult, possesses inalienable rights. All human beings are architects of their own personal and collective destiny by virtue of their own participation in that destiny. The right to be thus is of the very essence of human nature, which is freedom and creativity.

When liberty is denied or creativity is blocked, and society prevents any worthwhile initiative in private or public life, human beings suffer profound frustration. Nothing can replace freedom and creativity: neither material goods nor an abundance of cultural benefits nor the promise of eternal life. Human beings prefer to go without bread rather than surrender their freedom. Bread eaten in conditions where oppression is tolerated is bitter and dishonorable.

Militancy, the fruit of passion and mystical enthusiasm, gathers force when it arises from direct contact with those whose basic rights have been violated. Then we see clearly that militancy has more to do with actual human beings than with ideas or ideals. But in the ruined lives and injured countenances of the deprived we nevertheless discern a secret dignity, a hidden incorrigible strength.

This is confirmation of the truth enunciated by faith: the humiliated and the injured are successors of the suffering servant Jesus Christ. Like the crucified Christ, they too wish to live and to rise again. In the progress which they make, in their movements and organizations, they proclaim the signs of the resurrection taking place in history, whenever the claims of a just life triumph over the interests of the privileged few.

God is the God of all human beings; God has demonstrated this existentially—this is the God of those who weep, of the loving kindness of the oppressed, of the revolution that will change the unjust order of this era, and of the new life offered to all men and women. To serve that cause in this world is to celebrate an authentic liturgy acceptable to God. The progress we make has a social and political but also an eternal significance, because it anticipates the imminent kingdom of God. A poet has written: "Sweeper sweeping the street, / You are sweeping in the kingdom of God." The activity of the humble streetsweeper is just an action of a certain kind, but to the eye of faith it is a political act. It forms part of the divine dispensation, the establishment of God's kingdom, the redemption and integral liberation of creation.

This mystical perspective has to prevail through any possible failures and setbacks, which are neither definitive nor the last word in history. Existence is inscribed within the circumference of a greater cause and within the assurance of Jesus' resurrection. That is the cause of life and of the radiant dimension of history. It also affects action, for it leads to a nonpolitical treatment of certain questions. Everything is indeed political, but politics is not everything, for human existence and social reality have other dimensions; they are characterized by subjectivity, gratuitousness, celebration, good humor, and play, all aspects that have to be integrated with politics.

How to Draw on Your Own Resources

Every living thing must be nourished. Thus we all have a sense of the mystery and mystical experience on which to draw.

Above all, time has to be set aside for contemplation and meditation. I am not thinking of meditation in the conventional sense of acts of recollection and interior reflection. Essentially, it is a matter of cultivating an attitude oriented to the creation and nourishment of a personal center. The center is built up slowly as one tries to summon up all possible inward energy and synthesize it with experience and finally with the inspirations that arise in the course of real life. For those who have developed their centers, facts are no longer mere facts but are always messages, values, and symbols that speak to subjectivity. Contemplation becomes a habit of mind and heart.

Contemplation focuses on life itself, the course of history, and the struggle of the impoverished. Many people find that contemplative reading of meditational classics (scripture, the Wisdom books, the psalms, the "Life of Chuang-Tzu," the "Tao-te-Ching," the "I Ching," *The Imitation of Christ*, Luther's "Freedom of a Christian," *The Divine Milieu* of Teilhard de Chardin, and so forth) enables them to become immersed in their center. For others, it is profound silence that allows them to create the inward space from which there rise, ultimately from the profound depths of the center, intuitions that serve to orient the spiritual life and improve their self-knowledge.

Second, it is important to create a discussion group with whom we can analyze ideas and thoughts, communicate experiences, and nurture the same dreams and the same basic life project. The importance of a discussion group resides in the confirmation of beliefs, the correction of errors, and the completion of our vision of things with an assurance of security in what we do and are. The discussion group should not descend to the level of the gratuitous or recreational—meeting only to eat or drink or merely for entertainment. It should promote serious discussion of basic questions involving destiny and the struggle for a better meaning to life.

Third, we should make a special place for prayer, the attitude of the soul when it opens up directly to God. It is one thing to think of God, to speak of God and of God's dispensation—that is what theology and religious discourse do all the time. It is a very different thing to speak to God, to open up to God, to complain to God of the excessive darkness of history, to ask again and again: When will it end? Why is it so, my God? There are so many tragedies in the lives of individuals and the poor the meaning of which is hidden in the depths of a divine plan which, in its turn, is concealed from us and which we cannot wholly reconcile with loving kindness, rejoicing, singing, and dancing before God in thanks for the superabundance of meaning, light, and satisfaction in life, and with our knowledge of love and our experience of fulfillment. To reach even that level of acceptance we have to live through a mystical experience and allow ourselves to be seized by mystery.

This is prayer, and prayer in this sense exalts us because it continually takes us out of ourselves and centers us in the absolute outside us, above us, and within us. This absolute proffers itself in the form of an absolute loving Other, whom we cannot tame or domesticate, but who gives freely to us and is always present for us, even when we are crucified by our problems. This is much more than a gesture. It enables us to identify God in the melée of things among which we might otherwise lose sight of God.

Fourth, celebration is fundamental. It is essentially communitarian. As Nietzsche said, celebrating is being able to say yes and amen to everything. In celebration the world is transfigured, for everything becomes symbol and sacrament. Celebration presupposes the capacity to remove ourselves from the conflicts of the world. When it appears it is like a liberation, a major drama which turns out all right in the end (it is the *felix culpa* of St. Augustine). In celebration we live out symbolically something that history actually denies us. Consequently, celebration has an irrefutably anticipatory nature. When celebrating we already sing of the victorious revolution, we already rejoice ritually at the achievement of liberation, and we already feel that we are sitting down to a banquet with God as guests or as sons and daughters in our Father's house.

Without celebration, which is accompanied by festivity, music, and aesthetic beauty, and by purification of body and mind (a feast is only festive when it is ready and waiting), mystery runs the risk of becoming a formula, and mysticism and mystique mere transient psychological uplift. In celebration it is as if everything—within and without, dream and reality, far and near, the world and God—has reached its culmination and point of convergence.

Fifth, we need to experience important occasions which become touchstones for us. Foundational moments are required to maintain the tone of mystique and the power of mystery. We need to concentrate mainly on this experience, to spend time on that, to isolate perfect moments, surroundings, and things that spur and inspire us (conversations, friends, meditations for times when we are alone, and for recollection and interiorization). These occasions and experiences are like springs which feed on mystery. Such beacons and irruptions into life enable us to keep alive the memory of mystery, always present yet so easily overlooked, in every warp and woof of our time.

We have to bring this mystical dimension of our life to bear on the community in which we work. Most people have some contact with what is essentially a mystical form of religion. It is apparent in the way in which they conceive the world and events, and see them as pervaded by divine providence. For many people God is not a religious category but forms part of the deepest experience of life. They do not believe in God, but they know existentially that God is there, in their natural assurance that the Lord and giver of life holds them close and sustains them.

We have to exchange experiences and to remain open to novelty if the community is to benefit from fresh elements. These often arise as the collective expression of a new religious awareness which finds expression in social movements that make room for and value the religious dimension (basic ecclesial communities, meetings of priests and workers, social pastorals and discussion groups of various churches on problems affecting blacks, the land question, Indians, housing, women, health, and so on). It is always enriching to learn of and from faith, hope, gestures of solidarity and true love, and the celebrative creativity of popular culture, because those whom God loves, the poor and marginalized, live and express themselves in these ways. It is often they who keep the divine light, the light of the sacred and of the Mystery behind human existence, burning as if in a sanctuary. It is they who ensure that the most decisive element in history is not weakened or lost.

To conclude, mysticism is life itself apprehended in its radicalism and extreme density. Existence is endowed with gravity, buoyancy, and depth when thus conceived and known appropriately. Mysticism always leads to the transcendence of all limits. It persuades us to examine other aspects of things than those we know and to suspect that reality is more than a mere structure concealing the realm of the absurd and the abyss, which can strike fear and anguish into our hearts. Mysticism teaches us instead that reality is where tenderness, receptivity, and the mystery of loving kindness can triumph and are encountered as joyful living, meaningful accomplishment, and a fruitful dream. This dream is of a universe of things and people joined together in brotherhood and sisterhood, firmly anchored in the heart of God, who is the Father and Mother of infinite goodness.

CHAPTER 9

Spirituality and Sex

A Radical View

There are two ways of approaching the theme of spirituality and sex.

The first is to look at both terms—spirituality and sex—as a twofold reality with certain natural similarities and differences, then to scrutinize them for compatibility, suggesting points of contact and divergence. This procedure has its own specific value. It is an attempt to grasp and understand a certain kind of experience in empirical terms and from the viewpoint of everyday life. It nevertheless conceives of spirituality and sexuality as essentially separate phenomena as far as our experience of them is concerned. This approach relies on a certain philosophical understanding, in other words a notion of reality that objectifies it as so many self-justifying data in need of no further explanation.

The second approach tries to see spirituality and sex as the result of a more profound vital process. Although in this view we may still think of reality as consisting of a number of concrete data, we may also see it as made up of various elements that are simultaneously aspects of a single, much deeper process. This more profound reality is always open. It is the latent force or power behind all the forms in which it may, as it were, become manifest.

From this viewpoint, sexuality and spirituality do not appear as immediate data but as the mediated results of a process. Their meaning is not obvious, for they hint at dimensions much more profound than those apparent in their immediate reality. They are not self-explanatory but call for an explanation.

Surely it is not too fanciful to think of spirituality and sexuality as manifestations of a single vital energy that runs through all human existence and in time emerges in those particular forms. Then our experience of them as dynamic realities would refer us eventually to the underlying dimensions and the ultimate power that is their substrate. I incline to this radical viewpoint.

With the first approach the notion of spirituality is relatively distinct. It is all that activity that may be attributed to the spirit or soul, conceived as distinct from and even opposed to the body. Then the human being is seen as a unitarian combination of body and spirit. Spirituality operates in one dimension of the human, that of the spirit. The spirit has such properties as reflection, inwardness, and contemplation. Spirituality enjoins the pacification of physical impulses, a calming of the senses, and the devotion of physical space to the concentrated attention of the spirit. A human being has to develop a certain degree of this "spirituality" to maintain the necessary equilibrium when faced with all the exaggerated and provocative demands that everyday life, and above all our culture, make on the physical senses.

In the same way, sexuality is another conceptually distinct and defined area. It is that dimension of human affectivity which is expressed through one person's opening up to another in erotic intimacy and genital intercourse. Seen thus, it is a universal energy giving rise to tensions that demand gratification. To be sure, to maintain its human dimension, and as the expression of communion between the sexes, sexuality also implies a certain kind of spirituality. In that perspective it is not difficult to make quite interesting connections between the two distinct areas of spirituality and sexuality. But this is not the approach that I should like to adopt. I prefer a less metaphysical approach, one which tends more to the notion of process and is even richer and more attractive, aiming as it does at identification of the common yet hidden roots of the two phenomena.

The Primordial Experience of the Spirit

The word *spirit* conceals a primordial experience to be found in the archaeology of the great religions and at the bases of Western and Oriental philosophy. We experience the spirit not as a mere part of the human being, but as a vital whole. *Spirit* is then the term for the energy and vitality of all manifestations of being human. In that sense spirit is not opposed to body, but includes it. The body is always vitalized, that is, spiritualized. Spirit is, however, opposed to death. The main contrast is not between spirit and matter, or between soul and body, but between life and death.

Spirituality in this sense means living according to the spirit, in accordance with the dynamism of life. It has to do with an existence oriented to the affirmation of life and to its protection and promotion. Here I mean life seen in its integrity, whether in terms of its outward aspects in, say, relations with others, with society and with nature, or in its inward aspects in, say, dialogue with the inner self, with the superior being that dwells behind us (in the world of archetypes). This dialogue is conducted by means of contemplation, reflection, and inwardness; in short, through the power of subjectivity.

That which makes life human and is characteristic of the human element of the spirit is to be found in the capacity for relations without discrimination, in acceptance of the other in all his or her distinctiveness, and in solidarity all the way to identification with the wholly other—with those others who are the suffering and unjustly marginalized. This human quality is, in short, disinterested love. Spirituality represents an authentic life project: living life as sensitivity to the nature of one's own life; affirming the lives of other human beings, especially those whose lives are unjustly diminished; and apprehending life in all its cosmic manifestations, from the primal movement of subatomic matter replete with energy and intentionality, all the way to fully realized forms of vegetable and animal life. The Hebrew Bible rightly says: "Therefore choose life, that you and your descendants may live" (Dt 30:19).

Death is contrasted with, opposed to, life; death, that is, not in the sense of the biological phenomenon of disintegration, but as a way of excluding others, as an inflation of the ego which interrupts communication with others, and as a misappropriation of the lives of others. Such a way of life produces not life but death in the sense of a bar to growth and to the development of existence and, in the end, leads to death for others.

I shall now look at the meaning of the spirit as life, for we have to understand life in order to appreciate the deep significance of spirituality.

We experience the spirit under two aspects, in an inward and in an outward form.

First we have inwardness. Here the spirit appears as the dynamism or thrust of the human psyche. It has various aspects or dimensions. It may be seen as profound, unconscious, archetypal, instinctive, mysterious, conscious, emotive, intellectual, and volitional. The spirit is a vital energy, which may be realized gradually throughout life, and which is channelled and manifests itself in the more varied forms of the imagination, consciousness, affectivity, and will. These actual manifestations are concentrated in the empirical self and, at a certain level, can be educated and controlled. This is the field of action of the personal force. Everything converges on our conscious self.

But this conscious self does not represent the ultimate reality. Instead, it refers to a deeper self located at the level of the personal and collective unconscious. Mystics and depth psychologists lay great stress on this deeper self (see, for instance, Léon Bonaventure's invaluable *Psychologie et mysticisme*.) A force emerges and a light breaks forth from the depths of the human psyche, and we become aware of a living and vital center that straightforwardly inspires or takes command of the empirical self. Mystics like Teresa of Avila called it "supernatural," which does approximate to the truth, though this force and center do not lie "outside" the human psyche. The force in question is the supreme expression of the psyche (and in that sense belongs to the natural realm). We call it supernatural because it imposes itself on that aspect of the natural that we term the conscious self. The conscious self is considered natural because we have it at our disposal and in a certain sense we are able to develop, even create it. But the reality which permeates the psychic life of the individual arises from something much deeper. Mere being is just given, just there, like that, and does not draw on individual or profound resources. Therefore the conscious self is of no account unless its supernatural aspect is influential and effective.

The incursion of the deeper self appears as the experience of a center on which everything converges, consciously or unconsciously; or as a sun which is the attractive center of a universe of psychic planets. It is encountered as something with qualities that declare it to be supreme, absolutely important, luminous, fascinating, and tremendous. These characteristics are typical of the experience of the sacred as described in the phenomenology of religion by anthropologists and others such as Rudolf Otto, Van der Leeuw, and Mircea Eliade.

The sacred does not reside primarily in reputedly sacred objects. The sacred is that dimension of profundity which bestows totality and unity on the psychic (or mental and psychological) life. In our culture, which is imbued with Judeo-Christian experience, there are constant references to the divine image (the *imago Dei*) or the image of God which shines forth from the center of our inward life and often takes the form of Christ. Meister Eckhart calls this the "divine spark," "the spark of the soul," or the "birth of God in the soul." (In other cultures the references are to other figures, such as Buddha, Atman, Krishna, and so on.) Everything is drawn toward this center. Everything is connected to it.

If by religion we mean the force that connects all human beings to their divine and sacred center and brings them together there, then we are all religious. We have to do here with a structure of the human psyche; with something authentically and truly instinctive; with, indeed, an innate mechanism which operates independently of conscious motivation; and with a constantly and regularly apparent impulse oriented to the very center of the individual.

This religious instinct spurs the individual to appropriate and master the self, and to unify the inward, higher, and outward worlds on the basis of a live and radiant center. The effect is one of deep peace, an undeniably integrative feeling and overwhelming conviction that all fear and anguish have been banished.

In a letter of June 13, 1948, to theologian R. G. Frei, Carl Jung said: "Every day I thank God for having allowed me to experience the divine Image in myself. . . . Thanks to this gesture of grace, my life has been endowed with meaning."

The image of God or Christ and the experience of the center are expressed in terms of forceful symbols and emerge with rich layers of affective and sensuous meaning. This makes religious services and celebrations so important for people. In this way the world nurtures its center and shapes the deep meanings that make life purposeful. All human beings find this heightened universe, the experiences and encounters which take on a symbolic character, supremely important. Deeply significant instances awaken the profound subjectivity of the individual and call forth the center. Modern civilization tends to occupy the individual's attention with a flood of imperious messages and demands. Or else unrelenting yet mundane needs so assault a person that he or she cannot find the center. Injustice in personal and social relations is a sure barrier to the disclosure or emergence of the center. Unjust processes are doubly inhuman. They force the oppressor to block fine impulses, to deny that the other is like him or her, and even to dehumanize the self (to lose his or her own center). Only thus can anyone objectify and violate the integrity of the other. Oppression is indeed a process of dehumanization (which blocks any illumination which may shine forth from the center), for the victim turns the violence suffered into negation in all aspects of life, at table, at home, in school, and in the very core of human dignity. A lack of concern for the inward realm of the sacred leads to violation of its outward aspect, the person. Moreover, systematic violation of the sacred aspect of the human individual destroys the way to the shrine of human inwardness. But the longing for and impulse to social and political liberation opens up another road to interior freedom, and vice versa. In fact, this is a single process of liberation where within and without are integrated and work in cohesion.

The deep religious instinct and the integrative capacity constitute a reality like any other authentic aspect of the psyche. This, however, is the most radical of such aspects. It is no luxury that has to be paid for with the cash of the privileged but the force behind and the magnet which attracts even the humblest individual's entire potential.

Experiencing this richness of human inwardness as a quest for and cultivation (culture) of the personal center is "spirituality." It is necessary to stress the nature of this experience, which is neither merely intellectual nor attributable only to the conscious power of religious adherence, expressed in terms of a doctrine or dogma. On the contrary, an objective religious adherence may represent a formidable barrier when, instead of showing forth the experience of the sacred, it falsely claims to substitute for it. The ability to articulate the experience of the supernatural is part of the deepest mechanism of the human being.

The experience of the center is a meeting of self with self, of the conscious self with the deeper self. It is tantamount to a dialogue (which goes beyond speech) between the totality of my inwardness and the totality of my outwardness. It is the experience of life in its density, agility, and gravity. It is a form of peace and calm that the most advanced techniques cannot offer. It is the experience of eternal life in time and of the fullness of time in every respect. This experience is the secret source of spiritual life. It is spirituality.

The spirit, to be sure, is apparent in an outward form. This is not another kind of spirit, but the spirit in another aspect. According to the image proffered by St. Teresa of Avila in her *Interior Castle*, it may be conceived as a castle viewed from outside; this interior castle is the soul at the center of which flourishes the tree of the spiritual life. Seen from without, the soul or spirit is in its exterior aspect, which is thus the other dimension of spirituality.

What happens to the spirit when it comes up against the reality by which it is surrounded? It encounters a deeply contradictory reality. On the one hand, a human person seems to live in social union and to behave consistently. The individual lives in accordance with nature, and his or her social relations are such as to assure a life which is dignified and enjoyable. In this case spirituality is living, participating, and communicating with the actual rhythms of life and a balanced existence.

On the other hand, the spirit also encounters the rupture of social union, class division, and the evidences of death. Inward unity is negated outwardly. How can spirituality take due effect in a situation of this kind? Above all, it reacts. The spirit reacts on the one hand by exhibiting a sacred anger at perversion, and on the other hand by expressing sympathy for the victims.

Protest and sympathy produce a resolve to struggle and to seek the liberation of reality. Consequently, a spirituality of liberation and struggle ensues, and spirituality takes the form of a desire and will to build just relations and to initiate a process of humanization so that human beings can realize their freedom and enjoy their own identity. But all this is the fruit of a project which unites inwardness and outward reality. In the previous chapter I referred to this as mysticism.

One of the exemplary historical figures in the search for this union was the German folk leader, reformer, and revolutionary Thomas Münzer (1490-1525), in the Reformation period. Luther had replaced the pope's authority with that of the Bible. Münzer, well versed in the tradition of German mysticism (he knew Meister Eckhart, Suso, and Tauler), put the main stress on the experience of faith in a living encounter with the God who addresses us, especially through the misery of this world. For him, the practice of self-transformation should be joined with that of the transformation of suffering. For Münzer, the union of the two constitutes true mysticism and authentic spirituality. Only if outward union is achieved, with the exchange of an evil for a good reality, will inward union occur and spiritual men and women result. This was an insight of great spiritual consequence. It has been taken up again and again, most recently within the theology of liberation, which tries to combine and articulate faith and political, mystical, and liberating action.

But we have to be realistic. Socio-historical reality is structural in nature. Alienation is far from short-lived. And the process of liberation will take just as long. But will human existence always remain alienated from its basic quest? In reality it is not like that.

Practice has a symbolic dimension. Humankind learns how to celebrate life and struggle in a secular, family, and religious environment and in secular, family, and religious terms. In this symbolic universe we try out, as it were, and experience in anticipatory form the positive conclusion of history. We live in symbolic wise the unity which should also be put into real and lasting practice. This means that the symbolic universe is of fundamental importance for the integration of the psyche. In our symbolic universe we inaugurate symbolically the new society, the new heaven, and the new earth, and the new man and woman who, for a moment, are sacramentally present in us. Spirituality feeds on the vast symbolic world and is generally expressed through symbols. We may say that to the extent that we create a symbolic universe we shall be spiritual, and vice versa. Without that language the spirit languishes and becomes sterile. Thus the spirit expresses its desire, and to a certain extent realizes and establishes the basis for the hope which will do its own work of feeding longing and nurturing dreams.

The Primordial Experience of Sexuality

The hermeneutic process I have used to examine the category of spirit may also be applied to that of sexuality. I shall now look at the different levels of sexuality.

First of all, there is the biological dimension of sex. Empirically speaking, we have cellular genetic sex (the chromosomal configuration of man and woman); gonadal genital sex (the specific sexual organs of man and woman; the ovaries of the woman and the testicles of the man); and hormonal sex (androgens for a man and estrogens for a woman).

But there is also anthropological sex (actual men and women as such, as sexually diverse and related beings), and ontological sex. We may consider sexuality as a mode of being (and consequently, ontological means having to do with being and not with our interpretation of being), which pervades all manifestations of the human. Everything done by man and woman is done in that they are man and woman.

Therefore sex is not something that a human being possesses but something that a human being *is* in a particular and ineradicable form. This ontological sexuality is expressed in terms of the feminine and the masculine aspects found in every human being. But, obfuscated by forms of mediation and tied to an analytical process, the human being fails to continue on the path toward an area of mystery which is always known and always to be known. What is the meaning of sexuality in the context of the mystery of human existence?

Everything seems to show that human reason is incapable of explaining the most profound and ultimate significance of sexuality, which is also wholly resistant to any ethical inquiry or to any other discipline which seeks to scrutinize it by some form of control or sublimation. Sexuality has to be represented in terms of myths and grand symbols, to which by nature it discloses itself more generously.

Ontological sexuality is a radical form of sexuality. It is to be found behind all kinds of manifestations of sexuality. This variety is called radical because it is like a microcosm at the root (*radix*) of the human being. It is there in the same way as a microcosm is certainly to be found within all macrocosms. It is the fundamental energy of human life and of all other kinds of life and motion in the universe.

Various cultures have represented it symbolically as a serpent or dragon (the winged serpent). Pierre Weil has described the multiform significance of the serpent and dragon as ancient symbols of vital energy (see his *Mysticisme de sexe*). A much earlier form of serpent is probably Uroboros in its various manifestations and circular form (the mouth swallows the tail in order to symbolize the unity of conscious and unconscious, of masculine and feminine, of the self and the world); otherwise, when extended, it shows its head and tail (the basic division of the human being between conscious and unconscious, between myth and reason, between man and woman, between heaven and earth, and so on) (see Neumann's classic work, *Die grosse Mutter*). In modern medical symbolism the same figure appears as two serpents encircling a winged stick, standing for the staff of life. In the tantric yoga of ancient Indian wisdom, this serpent (universal sexuality) underlies the human being. There, sexuality is the energy known as *kundalini* (or *parakundalini*), which is Sanskrit for "serpent energy." It is portrayed as a coiled snake at the base of our spinal column, calm and in abeyance but capable of arousal.

The outcome of its awakening may be fortunate or tragic. Here we have a representation of the arousal of that cosmic energy which is in everything and takes a human form in us. It passes up the spinal column until it surges to the top of the head. Yoga seeks to awaken the force of *kundalini,* to control its surges, to establish equilibrium between cosmic energy and personal energy, and thus to penetrate to the realm of freedom and awareness of totality (nirvana).

Once awakened, *kundalini* follows its upward path through various degrees of awareness and of integration with existence as a whole. It passes through the various energy centers of the human being. Yoga calls these centers *chakras.*

The first *chakra* is located in the pelvic plexus, the control center of the sexual organs. We must remember that cosmic energy appears as sexual desire, and life is understood as enthusiasm and expansion. If it stays at the level of this *chakra* and does not continue its upward path, it may result in dependence and obsessions with a dehumanizing effect on the individual.

The second *chakra* is found in the abdominal center (the hypogastric plexus), which oversees reproduction and secretion. This implies a higher level of life where the human project to which sexuality is directed is the generation and elevation of life.

The third *chakra* is situated in the umbilical center (the hypogastric or solar plexus). Here there is a special connection with cosmic energy, which joins umbilically with the human being. This is also the location of nutrition and life.

The fourth *chakra* is located in the cardiac plexus, which controls the vascular system. At the level of consciousness it signifies the principle of self and the process of individuation (creation of the personal center).

The fifth *chakra* is situated in the cervical plexus, which controls the respiratory system. Through breathing we receive and restore cosmic energy, and enter into the vital process of the universe.

The sixth *chakra* is found between the eyes. It is the medulla that controls the reflexive nervous system. In one sense it is our third eye, or the eye of knowledge of the whole.

Finally, the seventh *chakra* is located in the cranial center, where we find the pineal gland, which controls the cerebral and volitional nervous system. *Kundalini* is oriented to nirvana, to liberating illumination. When that occurs, integration with the whole ensues. We feel part of a whole and the whole experiences that part of itself which we are.

This upward striving is a manifestation of the one and identical vital energy. This is also known as spirit, or sexuality in the radical understanding. It is known as *prana* or *kundalini* in the yogic tradition.

Let us return to the notion of sexuality. The human sexual dynamism implies a process of upward movement and universalization. Sexual relations begin with the instinctive aspect, with the discharge of a tension, and the calm search for the opposite (the first three *chakras*). But then, obeying the internal thrust and drive toward expansion, the human being needs to experience a relationship of gratuitousness, of love (the heart *chakra*) and rich exchange (the cervical and pulmonary *chakra*). This implies an experience of deep knowledge resulting from communion (the *chakra* of the head, of the third eye). In short, sexuality bears the individual toward transfiguration, to the experience of integration with the whole, in a great cosmic fusion (the *chakra* of the pineal gland).

This entire process is a single movement of ascension and of manifestation of vitality. The process of achieving this integration is punctuated by firm checks on sex at the instinctive level. This is not a matter of reprimand, as it were, but of ensuring that the force is kept within its limits and within its relations with the other expression of cosmic energy. Only by ascending and not staying within those instinctive bounds will the transcendence of love and the ecstasy of totality be reached. This is an authentic experience of the profundity of life and of the spirit, as presented in the foregoing.

The symbolic expression of this radical energy, as I have already mentioned, is the serpent, represented, for instance, by the Egyptian god Bes, the lord of the land of Punt. There is an image of Bes in the Louvre which was studied by Pierre Weil (*Mysticisme de sexe*). The deity is shown with an erect penis and the serpent Uroboros at his feet, with a serpent's head issuing from them, and with his knees around its head and pineal gland. This is a three-dimensional expression of the meaning of *kundalini* in its various manifestations in human reality: man/woman replete with the serpent; full of spirit and full of life.

This cosmic energy is not confined to human beings. It exists in all forms of life. It illumines all elements of creation, in matter in motion and in the complex interactions of matter and subatomic energy. The reaction of human beings when confronted by universal *kundalini* is one of admiration, attraction, enthusiasm, and the fascination of feeling immersed in the universal womb, where all things are welcome.

In Christian tradition, as I have stressed elsewhere in this book, there is a category which explains human and cosmic vitality: the Holy Spirit. In the theology of the Western church the Spirit is almost obscured because of a quasi-human way of representing the deity (God as the Supreme Being and the Spirit as the third Person of the Trinity) rather than showing the Spirit as energy and relation. Orthodox tradition conceives of reality essentially as life, energy, and relation.

From this viewpoint, before all else the Spirit represents all relationship, life, creativity, and the inauguration of a new heaven and a new earth. The Spirit hovers above primordial chaos (Gen 1:1). The Spirit creates order, invades everything, moves, communicates and ascends, is manifest in the prophets and in all those overtures which favor the emergence of the new and of the as yet unproven. The Christian creed says that the Spirit is the "giver of life."

The theology of the Orthodox church (especially Gregory Palamas, 1296-1359) makes a distinction between the personality and energy of the Spirit. The operation of the Spirit is discerned in creation, in natural elements, and particularly in vital processes. Just as the Son becomes incarnate, so the Spirit dwells in creation. Through the Spirit God is immanent in the world and enables it to receive divine reality: "Indeed, it is in him that we live and move and have our being," says St. Paul with overwhelming accuracy when addressing the Areopagus, or council of the Greeks, in Athens (Acts 17:28).

In light of the foregoing, we may say that the Spirit's energy permeates human beings. The Spirit is revealed in various forms of vital energy and thus spiritualizes humankind. Only in this sense does Christian rhetoric regarding the human being as the temple of the Holy Spirit (1 Cor 3:16; 6:19) have any real meaning.

In this context, spirituality means the capacity to experience the Holy Spirit in all cosmic energy, vital energy, and in various forms right up to powerfully integrative illumination. This is not a matter merely of one of the *chakras* (of that, say, which is linked to the genital organs), or of the energy of the soul, but of all inward power and the enlivening of the entire human being. It culminates—when it is replete with radical cosmic energy—in communion with the Holy Spirit, the principle sustaining the rationality of all beings, and acting as if (as nuclear science teaches us), everything (even elementary subatomic particles) existed in others, through others, and with others, in a single universal relational network. Spirituality consists in tuning in to the Spirit dwelling in everything and everywhere, living the enthusiasm (which in Greek has a "god" in the middle: *en-theos-mos*), which makes this communication possible and allows it to pass through us and to reach the point of transcendence.

The Balance between Sexuality and Spirituality

As I said at the beginning of this section, from a radical viewpoint spirituality and sexuality are two different names for a single phenomenon. They are manifestations of a single energy, which surpasses human existence.

Logically we should be able to delineate this phenomenon's particular characteristics, just as we have differentiated the two aspects of spirituality and sexuality. This distinction is important, moreover, in order to avoid making reality seem all too homogeneous. Nevertheless, it is preferable to stress the identity underlying the differences. Without this identity, which is intrinsic to both aspects, we would run the risk of falling into metaphysics in the shape of descriptive and analytical science. In the perspective of global and unitarian experience, it is important to emphasize the utility of the joint implications of the phenomenon in its several aspects and not to succumb to any form of fragmented scientific discourse. This takes us into our own and the cosmic dimension of radicality, which is vital energy.

This energy is the force of communication, communion, and ascension in all directions. It constantly takes human beings toward an experience of transcendence, where they can surpass their own limits and become immersed in that diversity which enables them to develop in the dimensions of their humanity until they erupt into cosmic totality. This energy is all-embracing and leads to communion with the entire universality of people, nature, and cosmos, and with that absolute Otherness which is the Sacred itself, divinity, God. Sexuality and spirituality are the two faces of this radical energy (the Spirit and its energy, *kundalini*).

The challenge that we have to measure up to is one of integration. The problem is not limited to what we make of our sexuality-genitality, as an instinct heavily exploited by the social communication media of our civilization, apart from any general pursuit of affectivity, contemplation, and ecstasy. We have to consider what we do with our vital energy, with the calls from our vital center, with our impulse to ascend, and with the urgent summons from the Spirit. Humanization means acknowledging and welcoming this energy. Then spirituality will be fulfilled in everything that we do and are, if we are wholly integrated with what we do and with what we wish to be.

St. Teresa of Avila said that to be spiritual meant being whole: "If you are eating chicken, eat chicken! If you are fasting, fast!" In other words, if you are eating chicken, go ahead and eat with good cheer, but if you are fasting, fast in all seriousness. Being spiritual means doing whatever we do to the full and consistently, whether we look at the question empirically (eating chicken) or from a spiritual viewpoint (fasting).

Then we shall be in sympathy and alignment with the summons issued by reality as a whole. We shall also be replete with the Spirit, the cosmic power that unifies everything and allows everything to converge at a point ahead of and above our present state.

The Expectant People
of Jesus Christ

Jesus was born outside human society, far from home, among animals, and in a manger, "because there was no room for them in the inn" (Lk 2:7).

His mission is clear from the start: to stand up for the deprived and to identify with the excluded. Then, as now, they make up the great majority of humankind. All human beings, irrespective of their moral situation, have the great privilege of bearing Jesus Christ within themselves. They are the "stable" where the church is to be found. The bellies of the poor still give birth to the liberator of the world. They have a thousand faces.

In this country there are millions of abandoned infants, as many as the entire population of Central America. There are the "disabled," who have actually been mutilated in order to beg for their food. There are the psychopaths stuck away in the obscurity of their homes or in psychiatric hospitals. There are the victims of fate who roam our streets, urchins who survive by petty theft. There are children who sell their bodies for sex to support their families. There are thousands of women who can find no work; the only door society leaves open for them leads to prostitution. There are the forty million blacks who bear the stigmata of discrimination on their bodies. There are the Indians eking out a living far from the reserves from which they have been driven. There are the thousands upon thousands of landless people who, like Abraham, leave this country in search of one where they can find work. There are the peripatetic workers who are a source of cheap fuel for the capitalist machine. There are the impoverished workers who think they are privileged to be exploited within the profit system instead of clutching a social security card and claiming the pathetic hand-outs of state benefit.

All these poor and suffering folk are about as esteemed as garbage. They are the humiliated and insulted of our own history and times, the neglected and forgotten of our national memory. They do not exist as far as this world is concerned but are known only to God. They are the beloved of the Father, the God to whom they cry, the God who comes down to hear the protests and lamentation rising up from this earth, and then, having listened to them, decides to free the oppressed.

All our little brothers and sisters cry out: "We want to live! We want to be real human beings! Surely we too are sons and daughters of God? When, Lord, shall we come face to face with you and know your justice, your tender love, and your peace?"

At Christmas God leaves the remote recesses of the divine light and shines instead into the dark lives of the marginalized and victimized. God gathers in all the oppressed or, rather, identifies with them, telling them: "You are my favorite sons and daughters. For your sake I shall be Emmanuel, God with you. I shall wipe away all the tears from your eyes. I shall be the way you will take and the life you will lead. My name is Jesus, the Liberator-God."

God is truly God only as the God of those who are shut out. God is born for us at Christmas and whenever we imitate God and include all the excluded in our life and in our struggle. Only then will Christmas be "a great joy for all the people" (Lk 2:10).

Brothers and sisters, let us remember and defend our huts and cabins, our streets, our *favelas*, our poor. Let us recall and protect them with loving care, for we await the coming of Jesus Christ. He wishes to be born again in your option for the oppressed, in your struggle for freedom, in your sharing in the cause, struggle, and life of the people.

Index

Also in the Ecology and Justice Series

John B. Cobb, Jr., *Sustainability: Economics, Ecology, and Justice*

Charles Pinches and Jay B. McDaniel, editors, *Good News for Animals?*

Frederick Ferré, *Hellfire and Lightning Rods*

Ruben L.F. Habito, *Healing Breath: Zen Spirituality for a Wounded Earth*

Eleanor Rae, *Women, the Earth, the Divine*

Mary Evelyn Tucker and John Grim, *Worldviews and Ecology: Religion, Philosophy, and the Environment*

Denis Edwards, *Jesus the Wisdom of God: An Ecological Theology*

Jay B. McDaniel, *With Roots & Wings: Spirituality in an Age of Ecology and Dialogue*

Sean McDonagh, *Passion for the Earth*